75 Memorable Moments in Minnesota Sports

75 Memorable Moments in Minnesota Sports

Joel A. Rippel

Forewords by Harmon Killebrew and Sid Hartman

Minnesota Historical Society Press

www.mnhs.org/mhspress

The Minnesota Historical Society Press is a member of the Association of American University Presses.

Manufactured in Canada. Book design by Wesley B. Tanner/Passim Editions

10 9 8 7 6 5 4 3 2 1

∞ The paper used in this publication meets the minimum requirements of the American National Standard for Information Sciences—Permanence for Printed Library Materials, ANSI Z39.48-1984.

International Standard Book Number 0-87351-475-0 (cloth)

LIBRARY OF CONGRESS CATALOGING-IN-PUBLICATION DATA

Rippel, Joel A., 1956–
    75 memorable moments in Minnesota sports / Joel A. Rippel ; forewords by Harmon Killebrew and Sid Hartman.
        p. cm.
    ISBN 0-87351-475-0 (cloth : alk. paper)
    1. Sports—Minnesota—History. I. Title: Seventy-five memorable moments in Minnesota sports. II. Title.
    GV584.M65R56 2003
    796'.09776—dc21

                                                                      2003011667

*In loving memory of Verona Rippel;
for Jennifer, Emmalie, and Charlie*

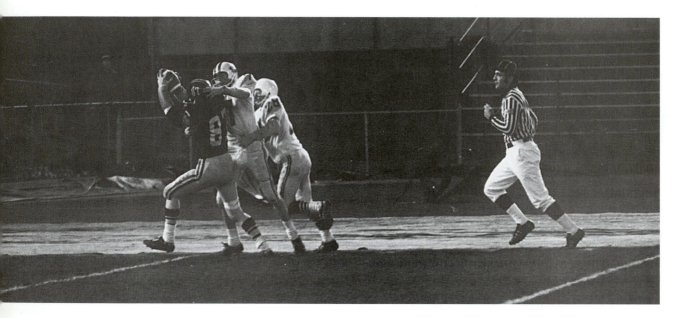

Table of Contents

Foreword

by Harmon Killebrew

In the fall of 1960, I was playing in Washington, D.C., with the Senators when they told us we were moving to Minnesota. I have to admit, I wasn't very excited about the move. We were just starting to become a good ball club in Washington, and I felt our loyal fans deserved to see a winner. And I really liked playing in the nation's capital—with the excitement of meeting all the presidents, congressmen, senators, and other famous people who attended our games. At that time, I really didn't know much about Minnesota. I had played in the American Association with Indianapolis for about a month in 1958, so I'd traveled to St. Paul and Bloomington and I knew what the weather would be like. I just wasn't sure that was where I wanted to go. I wasn't looking forward to playing baseball in that kind of stuff.

But when we got there, boy, I tell you, the people were so wonderful, such great fans—they just embraced us. And, of course, as Joel relates in these pages, our young players had time to develop and we became a winning ball club. In the end, I was happy that Minnesota was where I played my career, because the people there were my kind of people. With my personality—and as someone who came from a small town in Idaho—Minnesotans were people I could relate to.

I have so many memories from Minnesota that it's hard to pick any one moment. Paging through this book, I see Joel has chosen many favorites that are on my list. Being a Twin meant that I had the opportunity to play on a lot of great ball clubs and with some talented players over the years. Just putting on that uniform and walking onto the Met Stadium field to represent the Twins was about as big a thrill as anything for me. But the most memorable moment, of course, was when we won the pennant in '65. And hitting the home run just before the All-Star break that put us five games in front of the Yankees. Probably our strongest team was the one we fielded in '69. We had Cesar Tovar leading off, Rod Carew batting second, Tony Oliva and me alternating at third and fourth. That was my best year in baseball—49 homers and 140 RBIs.

For me, it's still a thrill to come back to Minnesota, to see the people and talk to them. Fans are always bringing up particular games and saying stuff like, "Boy, wasn't it great to go out Saturday morning and be part of knothole games?" I've had farmers from North Dakota tell me they always listened to our games when they were out working in the fields.

All these recollections—memories held by the players and memories treasured by the fans—are so important. We've gotten away from it today, but I think that's what baseball should be about—memories of good seasons and great players. And that's what you'll find in *75 Memorable Moments in Minnesota Sports*. Joel really hit a grand slam with this book. It's a winner.

Foreword

by Sid Hartman

I can fondly recall many of the events Joel describes in this fine book. In 1944, Dick Cullum hired me as an intern for the *Minneapolis Times:* I've been following the Minnesota sports scene ever since. I started writing a column in 1946, but the *Times* folded in 1948 and I went to work for the *Minneapolis Tribune.* My first by-line in the *Tribune* appeared in May 1948, just days before Roy Campanella broke the color barrier in the American Association.

Those days were fun, mostly because of the rivalry between the Minneapolis Millers and the St. Paul Saints. In the 1930s and 1940s, the highlights of the holidays—Memorial Day, Independence Day, and Labor Day—were the double-headers between the Millers and the Saints. There would be a morning game at either Nicollet Park in Minneapolis or Lexington Park in St. Paul and an afternoon game at the other stadium. Seventeen members of the Baseball Hall of Fame played for the Millers, including Ted Williams, Willie Mays, Ray Dandridge, Hoyt Wilhelm, and Carl Yastrzemski. Campanella and Duke Snider played for the Saints.

But the two biggest things on the Minnesota sports scene following World War II were Gopher football and the state high school basketball tournament. The Gophers were the kings of college football when they won five national titles between 1933 and 1941, but a Gopher football game was even bigger after World War II. People had more money, the whole atmosphere in the Twin Cities and the country was electric, and it carried over to Gopher football. The next biggest thing through the fifties was the state basketball tournament. When teams from places like Edgerton, Lynd, and Walnut Grove made it to Williams Arena, people went crazy.

The state has been home to a number of memorable professional teams as well. The Minneapolis Lakers and George Mikan were the dominant team in pro basketball from 1947 to 1954—winning one NBL championship and five NBA championships in that span. And in 1961, major league baseball and football finally came to the Twin Cities. The Minnesota

Twins won the American League title and played host to the All-Star Game in 1965, but the moment everyone remembers from that year came two days before the All-Star Game. The first-place Twins were playing the New York Yankees, who had won four consecutive A.L. titles, on a Sunday afternoon at Met Stadium. With the Twins down by two in the ninth, Harmon Killebrew hit a long home run to win the game. Ray Scott was the play-by-play announcer for WCCO-radio, and the station must have replayed his call of that home run five thousand times in the years since then.

Bud Grant took the Vikings to the Super Bowl after the 1969 season, his third year on the job. Suddenly, the Twin Cities and the state belonged to the Vikings. It stayed that way for a long time.

All of these stories and more are told in *75 Memorable Moments in Minnesota Sports.* Whether these are moments you remember fondly or events you're learning about for the first time, you're sure to enjoy the experience. This book brought back a lot of great memories for me.

Preface & Acknowledgments

During the 2000 major league baseball season, the Minnesota Twins asked fans to vote on their favorite moments from the team's forty seasons, and in August the team announced the top ten. Kirby Puckett's heroics in game six of the 1991 World Series was picked as the number one moment in team history. Seven of the other nine moments on the list were from 1987 or later. All of the events on the list were noteworthy and deserving of recognition, but they started me thinking about great moments from the Twins' first twenty-six years in Minnesota that didn't make the list.

Long a fan of "where are they now?" features and "this date in history" items, I was inspired to compile my favorite Minnesota sports memories. While assembling this list, I stuck to what I know: traditional spectator sports. This is not to imply that "non-spectator" activities such as hunting and fishing or winter sports like curling, skiing, and speed skating aren't memorable. Those activities are a big part of Minnesota's sports history, which dates to pre-statehood days. Lacrosse was played at Fort Snelling as early as 1836, and there were boxing matches taking place in the state beginning in 1876. More recent events like the Twin Cities and Grandma's Marathons are a big part of the Minnesota sports scene, though they are not noted within these pages.

Any list of "memorable" sports events is subjective. Having been a sports fan for as long as I can remember, I have my own favorite recollections. One of my top memories is also one of my earliest. In 1970, Sherburn, located just eight miles from my hometown of Trimont, won the state basketball tournament. That event is one of the chapters in this book.

When I was a sophomore in high school, I started working for my hometown weekly newspaper—the *Trimont Progress*. I've been connected with newspapers ever since. Working in the sports department has allowed me to combine my vocation with my avocation. It's also allowed me to gain a broad knowledge of the Minnesota sports scene. I've tried to balance the list that makes up this book between the exciting events that create indelible memories for the sports fan and the events that have a lasting effect on our state's history. My choices are certainly open to debate. But that's the fun in writing a book like this.

Thinking about these "memorable moments" allows us to relive them, with all their excitement and drama. I hope you, the reader, feel the same enthusiasm I did as I

researched and wrote this book. And I hope it spurs you to create your own list of memorable moments in Minnesota sports.

This book grew out of an idea I presented to Greg Britton of the Minnesota Historical Society Press. He and Kevin Morrissey were enthusiastic about the project from the start and improved my original idea. Editor Shannon Pennefeather kept the project in focus. Sally Rubinstein and Deborah Swanson of the Minnesota Historical Society Press were very helpful.

Brian Wicker of the Star Tribune gave me valuable input and was generous with his time.

I am grateful to the staffs of the News Library of the Star Tribune, the Minnesota Historical Society library and microfilm room, and the University of Minnesota Archives; and Michelle King, Jerry Lee, and Karen Zwach of the athletic media relations office at the University of Minnesota.

I would also like to thank Anders Gyllenhaal, Bob Jansen, and Peter Koeleman of the Star Tribune; Bill Robertson and Jason Ball of the Minnesota Wild; Dan Bell of the Minnesota Timberwolves; Mike Cristaldi of the Minnesota Lynx; Molly Gallatin and Brad Ruiter of the Minnesota Twins; and Howard Voight and Ann Johnson of the Minnesota State High School League.

75 Memorable Moments in Minnesota Sports

August 15, 1857

Play Ball!

Baseball Arrives in Minnesota

One year before Minnesota became a state, a Philadelphia lawyer arrived on the banks of the Mississippi River a few miles downstream from St. Paul with a dream of building a model community.

Prior to moving to the territory, Ignatius Donnelly began publishing a newspaper called the *Emigrant Aid Journal,* in which he urged Philadelphia's European immigrants to relocate to his village in Minnesota Territory. Platted just west of Hastings in Dakota County in summer 1856, the town was named Nininger. Donnelly, twenty-six at the time, and real estate tycoon John Nininger, the brother-in-law of Alexander Ramsey, the territory's first governor, had big dreams for their town. One was to build a railroad—the Nininger and St. Peter Western Railroad—to carry grain from central Minnesota to the Mississippi River. Another priority was to establish a baseball team.

In its August 1, 1857, issue the *Emigrant Aid Journal* invited those citizens of Nininger "in favor of forming a Base Ball Club" to a meeting held two days later in the newspaper's office: "Our young friends who delight in athletic sports, will now have an opportunity of enjoying this interesting and invigorating game so much played in the Eastern cities. We hope to see such a club here as may provoke to emulation and competition the young men of surrounding towns, when matches and return matches will be played to the gratification of assembled thousands. Why not?"

On August 15, the newspaper notified its readers that a game would be played that afternoon at 3 P.M. on the "lower addition" and that it wasn't too late to join the team. The fee for those interested in joining the club, whose president was G. H. Burns and secretary was Charles Ledie, was twenty-five cents.

Two weeks later the *Emigrant Aid Journal* did not mention the result of the August 15 contest—the first baseball game in state history—but its September 12 issue reported that the town's team was gaining notoriety: "The Nininger Base Ball Club is becoming noticed

One county to the south and seventeen years after the first baseball game was played in Nininger, the Shattuck School baseball club of Faribault posed for a team photograph.

abroad. We see an account of one of its games has been given in the first sporting paper of the day, *Porter's Spirit of the Times,* we understand it is designed by the Club to challenge other towns, shortly, to play them a match game. They meet every Saturday afternoon for play on their grounds, on the lower addition."

But Donnelly's grand experiment and the community were short-lived. He was unable to secure backing for his railroad after a financial panic in 1857 inspired a three-year depres-

OUR·NINE

Baseball quickly matured into America's pastime, and advertisements like this 1880s cigar label capitalized on the sport's popularity.

sion. Nininger went into gradual decline and eventually became a ghost town. The town's solitary contribution was bringing baseball to Minnesota. By summer 1859, the game made its way upstream to St. Paul. After the Civil War, the number of teams in the state dramatically increased, and, just a decade after that first game—on September 24, 1867—the St. Paul North Stars won the first state baseball tournament.

July 22, 1891

A Boxing Showdown

Governor Cancels World Championship Bout

Early in 1891, two Minnesota promoters attracted nationwide attention when they announced they would stage a world middleweight championship boxing match in St. Paul that summer. As it turned out, this match was a fatal attraction for the sport in Minnesota.

At the time, it was natural that the state would play host to a boxing match of national interest. Ever since the first professional bout in Minnesota—held in Winona in 1871—the state had enjoyed a prominent role in the development of the sport nationwide. During the 1880s, some of the greatest fighters in the country—including legendary heavyweight champion John L. Sullivan—fought in Minneapolis. And in February 1891, one of the longest matches in boxing history took place in Minneapolis. Danny Needham of St. Paul finally won the battle when he knocked out Tommy Ryan of Syracuse, New York, in the seventy-sixth round. The fight, held at the Twin City Athletic Club (a small arena on Hennepin Avenue between Fifth and Sixth Streets), followed the Marquis of Queensbury rules—three-minute rounds with one minute of rest in between. The fight lasted more than five hours.

Three months later, Australian Bob Fitzsimmons, winner of three world titles (middle, heavy, and light heavyweight), fought and won a match in Minneapolis. While Fitzsimmons was in town, Minneapolis and St. Paul papers announced he would fight Australian rival Jim Hall—the only fighter to beat Fitzsimmons before he came to America—on July 22 in an outdoor arena on West Seventh Street in St. Paul.

The anticipated match earned so much national publicity that it aroused reformers in Minnesota who wanted to make boxing illegal. At first Governor William R. Merriam refused demands to stop the fight, saying he wouldn't interfere. But the citizens continued to pressure Merriam, who was in his second two-year term as governor, even threatening to impeach him. The day before the fight, Merriam addressed a committee representing a

JACK DEMPSEY
HEAVYWEIGHT CHAMPION

GEORGE A. BARTON
REFEREE

BILLY MISKE

Minneapolis newspaperman George Barton officiated more than twelve thousand bouts, including this one in 1918 between Jack Dempsey and St. Paul's Billy Miske.

group of three hundred gathered at the capitol. According to committee member Archbishop John Ireland—whose description of prizefighting as "brutal" had been quoted earlier in the week by the *Minneapolis Tribune*—the occasion was a solemn one.

As reported by the *Minneapolis Tribune*, Merriam told the group, "I doubt, however—and the doubt has been strengthened by consultation with legal gentlemen—that I have the authority to interfere in this matter, except in the case of riot, where it has been shown municipal authorities have not the ability to enforce the law. I will consult with the attorney general in the matter and do what is in my power."

The committee urged the governor to at least issue a proclamation condemning the fight. Later that day, Merriam announced that the fight would violate a state statute that banned prizefighting—passed two years earlier and ignored to this point—and decreed that

the match should not be held.

The promoters insisted the fight would go on.

While the governor met with the reformists, another significant event was unfolding. Fitzsimmons and his trainers, who were staying in White Bear Lake, were served with warrants for their "intent" to break the law. Late in the afternoon, Fitzsimmons posted a five-hundred-dollar bond in St. Paul municipal court as a promise to "keep the peace." His trainers each posted two-hundred-dollar bonds.

Thomas Cochran Jr., one of the most vocal critics of the fight, responded to a reporter from the *Minneapolis Tribune*, who asked if the action to stop the fight had been undertaken at an unduly late hour: "I am frank to admit that something should have been done before. But that is no reason why we should let it pass without protest, nor

Governor William R. Merriam was at the center of a controversy over boxing in 1891.

why we should not do our utmost to stop it. Do these gentlemen hold that because they have heard of no public sentiment against the violation of the law that they consider themselves free to violate it? That seems to me to be a weak argument. I am heartily in sympathy with anything that is good in athletic sports. The fact there was no public complaint against prize fights in the past is no good argument for failing to go on the record now."

On the morning of the fight, Ramsey County sheriff Ed Bean asked the governor if he wanted the fight stopped. Answering affirmatively, the governor added that he would call out the National Guard, if necessary, to enforce the statute against prizefighting. By early afternoon, the fight's promoters agreed to cancel the fight. Frank N. Shaw told the *Minneapolis*

Tribune: "We have canceled the fight in order to prevent riotous proceedings, as the steps taken by the citizens opposing the contest would undoubtedly have led to bloodshed. We are for peace; they are for bloodshed and we want the people to understand it." Shaw and his partners refunded the advance gate, estimated at twenty-five thousand dollars.

The announcement of the cancellation quickly spread through Minneapolis and St. Paul as Twin Cities newspapers put out extra editions with bulletins. At 6:30 P.M., the First Regiment of the state militia took up posts around the athletic club. By 9 P.M. an estimated crowd of ten thousand had gathered, but no violence occurred overnight.

In the next session of the legislature, at the urging of Merriam, a law was passed making prizefighting a felony. In fact, boxing was banned in Minnesota until 1915. (The reform movement wasn't unique to Minnesota—by the early 1900s, boxing was legal in only three states: California, Nevada, and Louisiana.) But the ban didn't completely stop boxing in Minnesota. George Barton, a Minneapolis newspaperman for over fifty years and a boxing referee who officiated more than twelve thousand bouts, related in his autobiography, published in 1958, "The passage of the anti-prizefighting bill was followed by nearly a quarter-century of illegal 'sneak' fights."

A referee of many of these fights, Barton said they were conducted in tiny gyms in Minneapolis and St. Paul, in barns, and in the wooded areas along the Mississippi and St. Croix Rivers. So the matches wouldn't attract attention from the authorities, purses were small and fights were promoted by word of mouth. So, in the end, the reformers' efforts to abolish prizefighting in the state weren't totally successful, but they did force the promoters and the participants underground for more than twenty years.

June 1893
Town and Country Tees It Up

State's First Golf Course Built

Golfing in Minnesota got its start almost as an afterthought.

In June 1893, the Town and Country Club in St. Paul—formed five years earlier as a social club centered on the St. Paul Winter Carnival—was looking to boost its declining membership by supporting summer pastimes such as lawn tennis, croquet, and picnics. When a society reporter for the *St. Paul Dispatch* interviewed William F. Peet—one of the club's founding members, along with James J. Hill and Lucius P. Ordway—Peet mentioned at the end of the conversation that the reporter should write about golf, which at the time was virtually unknown in the Midwest. In his next column, the reporter noted that the club, described by the *Minneapolis Sunday Tribune* as "perhaps the most exclusive club of Twin City Society," was thinking of building a golf course.

The newspaper account drew the interest of Scottish golf enthusiast George W. McRee, who contacted Peet to offer assistance in building a course on Town and Country's grounds, located on the eastern banks of the Mississippi River near the Marshall Avenue–Lake Street bridge. After mulling it over, Peet decided golf might be a good thing for the club.

Peet and McRee—and the club's yardman—went to work, mowing what became the first golfing green west of New Jersey. (The first golf course in the United States was St. Andrews Golf Club in Yonkers, New York, which opened in November 1888.) Town and Country's first course, consisting of nine holes, was laid out on flat terrain atop a hill on an adjoining farmer's field. The holes were marked by tomato cans for the cups and fishing poles with red rags for the flags.

The sport didn't immediately catch on at the club. Initially, Town and Country's executive committee was reluctant to give Peet the fifty dollars he requested for more permanent equipment: cups to replace the tomato cans and flags in exchange for the fishing poles. According to Town and Country's history (published in 1988), the chairman refused on the

St. Paul's Town and Country Club was formed in 1888 as a social club centered on the Winter Carnival. In 1893, it became home to the first golf course west of New Jersey.

grounds that golf was a "dammed silly game." Years later, Peet recalled that some members "were very loath to believe golf was needed or could possibly last." Eventually the committee chairman relented and granted Peet's fifty-dollar request, and just weeks after Peet's offhanded remark to a local reporter, golf in Minnesota was born. That summer, about a dozen members dabbled in golf at the club. In summer 1894—the year the United States Golf Association, the national governing body for the sport, was formed—two or three dozen members regularly played at Town and Country.

The club used its nine-hole course for the better part of five years before redesigning and expanding its course to eighteen holes. The revamped course opened on June 9, 1898. A year later, Minneapolis gained its own course when the Minikahda Club, located off Excelsior Boulevard overlooking Lake Calhoun, opened. The first round of golf at Minikahda was played on July 15, 1899.

Originally focused on the St. Paul Winter Carnival, Town and Country had established itself at the forefront of a decidedly non-winter sport. Today the club boasts the oldest course west of New Jersey and the nation's second oldest continuously played links.

The Minikahda Club, overlooking Lake Calhoun, was the second golf course to open in Minnesota. The first round of golf at the club was played on July 15, 1899.

February 24, 1900

Shooting Stars

Women's Varsity Plays First Basketball Game

In 1891, James Naismith's invention—a sport to fill the void between football and baseball seasons—didn't catch on with its intended audience, male college students, because they didn't think it was manly enough. Their female counterparts, however, quickly became enamored of basketball. The University of Minnesota was no exception. After the game was introduced to Minnesota women in 1893 by Max Exner, a former roommate of Naismith's, it quickly spread from Carleton College in Northfield to Minneapolis, where fifty University of Minnesota students formed a women's basketball association in early 1897.

Three years later—on February 24, 1900—the University of Minnesota's women's varsity played its first game against an outside opponent, welcoming a team from Stanley Hall, a Minneapolis prep school for young women, to the north wing of the Armory. Only women were admitted to the game, paying twenty-five cents for their tickets. According to the *Ariel,* a student publication that preceded the *Minnesota Daily,* "Stanley Hall was out in force with horns and color and was most confident of success, but when time was called at the end of the second half, the score was against them, 12–6. Both sides played a hard, fast game. Stanley Hall was better in guarding and in team play, but the individual work of the 'U' girls was way ahead."

Over the next eight seasons, the University's women's basketball team was one of the best in the country. During that period, the varsity team often played in front of a full house in the 992-seat Armory gym and routinely traveled out of state, playing games in Nebraska, North Dakota, and Wisconsin. The women dominated their opponents—a mixture of Minneapolis and St. Paul high school and college teams—winning 46 of 51 games. In one five-year stretch, Minnesota won 36 of 37 games. During the 1902–03 season, the University's team, captained by Emily Johnston, went 9–0 and was named state champion by the *Minneapolis Tribune.*

The *University of Minnesota Alumni Weekly* offered this praise of the 1902–03 team: "perhaps there has never been a team representing the University in any line of sport that has shown such finished team work through so much of the season. The great beauty of the season's work has been the fact that five young women on the team always played as though controlled by a single purpose, to make the best showing possible." High praise indeed, considering that the previous season the Gopher men's team went 15–0 and its members were named national champions by the Helms Athletic Foundation.

During the 1903–04 season, the women's team played a home-and-home series with the University of Nebraska. After beating Nebraska 30–22 in Minneapolis, the team traveled to Lincoln, where the Cornhuskers won 30–18. Despite the loss, which was the Gophers' last for nearly four years, team captain Elizabeth Cox, who played high school basketball at Minneapolis Central, told the *Minnesota Alumni Weekly*, "We were entertained handsomely. The grand impression made by the Nebraskans will long be remembered."

By 1906, however, opposition to women playing intercollegiate sports was mounting. The *Minnesota Alumni Weekly* reported in its January 15, 1906, issue that Maria Sanford, a professor at the university from 1881 to 1909 once described as "the best known and best loved woman in the state," had attended a meeting of the Council of Deans and Advisors of Women in State Universities in Chicago over the Christmas break. Among the things agreed to by the council was that "physical training should be required of all women students for at least one year." But a majority of conference attendees were opposed to intercollegiate or public athletic contests for women.

According to Joanne Lannin, author of *A History of Basketball for Girls and Women*, basketball was creating such a controversy by 1908 that parents were forbidding their daughters from taking part. The Athletic Union, the national body that governed sports outside of high schools and colleges, declared it would not permit girls to play basketball games in public places because such displays spawned undesirable traits and led to the exploitation of women.

The 1907–08 season was the last official one for the Gopher women's team. In March 1908, the Minnesota team again traveled to Lincoln, where Minnesota defeated Nebraska 28–22. On April 4, the teams had a rematch in Minneapolis, which Nebraska won 9–3. That game was the final "intercollegiate" game for both teams until 1973. On April 24, 1908, the University of Nebraska Board of Regents, responding to concerns of faculty members who considered such activity inappropriate, abolished intercollegiate athletics for women. The following January, the University of Minnesota apparently reached the same conclusion. Though records are scant, a brief three-paragraph story in the *Minnesota Daily* in January 1909 announced that women's basketball would be restricted to intramural play. Despite the announcement, the women's varsity played two games that winter—against the School of Agriculture and Stanley Hall.

No public explanation for the sudden demise of "varsity" basketball for women at the

Women's basketball action took place in the north wing of the University of Minnesota Armory.

University was given and the disappearance mysteriously came fifteen years before women's education groups—such as the Women's Division of the National Amateur Athletic Foundation (founded by Lou Henry Hoover, wife of President Herbert Hoover)—openly criticized what they viewed as commercialism in sport, causing even intramural basketball for women to decline in popularity.

"Basketball for women did actually disappear in colleges faster than it did in high schools," noted Lannin. "The pressure was coming from physical education directors at colleges for women to just play intramural. That happening filtered down to high schools as all of those P.E. majors started their high school teaching careers."

After the mid-1920s, girls' basketball survived at a few high schools in Minnesota and in only a handful of rural states like Iowa, Texas, Oklahoma, and Maine. At the University of Minnesota, there were other factors for the sport's quick demise, including reports that university president Cyrus Northrop didn't like the women's team traveling out of state because the team required chaperones. One newspaper account told of dissension between the Min-

Women's basketball grew in popularity at the University of Minnesota in the early 1900s. The 1908 squad posed for a team portrait.

neapolis and St. Paul members of the team, which almost caused one season to be canceled. Or finances could have played a part: all of the University's athletic teams, under the direction of the Athletic Board of Control, were expected to be self-sufficient, but women's basketball, despite its popularity, apparently wasn't a moneymaker because of the guarantees that had to be paid to opposing teams. Another contributing factor may have been the overcrowded Armory gym, used by every athletic and military drill team and considered the University's town hall. A separate women's gymnasium—Norris Hall—wasn't built until 1915. Or other schools may have shut down their programs as the University of Nebraska did, leaving the 'U' with no intercollegiate foes to challenge.

Whatever the reason, it would be more than sixty years before varsity basketball for women returned to the University of Minnesota campus.

The Little Brown Jug

Gopher Football Comes of Age

While the first two decades of football for the University of Minnesota didn't generate much enthusiasm in the general public or student body, this apathy evaporated after the arrival of Dr. Henry Williams in fall 1900. Williams, an All-American football player at Yale and graduate of the University of Pennsylvania medical school, was Minnesota's first full-time, salaried coach, and he quickly put the Gopher football team in the public eye. The Gophers went 10–0–2 in his first season, 9–1–1 in 1901, and 9–2–1 in 1902. But these winning records were just a prelude to what happened in 1903. The Gophers opened the season with ten consecutive victories, outscoring their opponents 506–6. This heady success left the Gophers wondering how they compared with some of the best college football teams in the country.

They had a chance to test their mettle on October 31, 1903, when the University of Michigan football team came to Minneapolis riding a 29-game winning streak. That record, fueled by the Wolverines' potent offense—which averaged 56 points per game during that span—earned Wolverines' coach Fielding H. Yost the nickname "Hurry Up." The Wolverines had outscored their opponents over the previous two and one-half seasons 1,631–12. In their first seven games of 1903, the Wolverines had outscored their opponents 447–0.

The media's enthusiasm for the game was encapsulated by the *Minneapolis Tribune*'s Frank Force: "Men of Minnesota, the day of the championship contest is at hand." About twenty thousand fans jammed into Northrop Field to watch the contest, which started at 2:30 P.M.

After a scoreless first half, the Wolverines grabbed the lead when Willie Heston scored on a one-yard run. With time running out, it appeared that the Wolverines would hang on. But with just a few seconds remaining, Minnesota's Egil Boeckman scored to tie the game— his touchdown the only points allowed by the Wolverines the entire season.

The 1903 University of Minnesota football team, which included future College Football Hall of Famer Bobby Marshall (second row from top, fourth from left), battled powerhouse Michigan to a 6–6 tie.

Headlines the following day in the *Minneapolis Sunday Tribune* captured the mood: "Minnesota Supreme in Western Football," "Victory, though the score is tied," and "Yost and Michigan Practically Beaten." The *Tribune's* Force wrote: "Minnesota, Minnesota, Minnesota. You have reason to feel proud today, for yesterday eleven of your sturdiest sons won honor for themselves and you. . . . Not a victory in the score, for this stands but for a tie. A tie it will be counted in the football records of the year. But in the minds of those who saw the contest, the Minnesota-Michigan game at Northrop Field, October 31, 1903, will be considered one of the greatest victories Minnesota ever won. . . . Michigan the mighty has fallen."

Besides the tremendous football game—Michigan won its next 26 games to stretch its unbeaten streak to 56—another incident made this an extraordinary day. In their haste to leave the field as dusk was approaching, Yost and the Wolverines left behind their water jug. Early the next morning, equipment manager Oscar Munson found the jug, filled with Michigan spring water, near the Wolverines' bench. Munson took the jug to the office of L. J. Cooke, the head of the athletics department, and said in his heavy Scandinavian accent, "Yost forgot his yug." Munson then asked, "Shall I take the yug over to Yost at the West Hotel?"

Cooke replied, "No. If Yost wants it, let him come and get it."

Later that day, Cooke mentioned the jug to Williams, who said, "tell you what we'll do, L. J. We'll keep it and I'll advise Yost he'll have to win the jug if he wants it back."

The jug was painted with the words "Michigan Jug—

University of Minnesota equipment manager Oscar Munson's discovery of Michigan's water bottle helped create one of the most famous trophies in college football – the Little Brown Jug.

Captured by Oscar, October 31, 1903" and the score of the game. With that, one of the most famous football trophies in America was conceived. Williams wrote a friendly letter to Yost, telling him the Wolverines would have to win the jug back. The Gophers kept the jug for six years because the teams didn't meet again until 1909. But the Wolverines won that game, 15–6, and promptly repossessed their jug.

Pudge Calms the Crowd

Umpire under Siege at Millers Game

By midseason 1906, the American Association pennant race was heating up, and a feud was brewing in Minneapolis. In July, the Minneapolis Millers, under manager Mike Kelley, won ten consecutive games to pull within six and one-half games of the first-place Columbus Senators. With the Senators coming to Nicollet Park for a four-game series, the Millers had the opportunity to close the gap. For the crucial series, American Association president Joseph D. O'Brien assigned twenty-one-year-old Brick Owens as the solitary umpire.

Kelley and Owens had already had several run-ins during the first three months of the season, but they were nothing compared to what happened on and after July 18.

A raucous crowd of thirty-five hundred showed up for the series opener. The Senators opened the scoring with a run in the third inning, but the Millers tied the game in the seventh. The controversy originated in the next inning, when Owens called two Millers out at the plate on successive plays—"two of the rawest decisions to ever go against the Millers," in the words of the *Minneapolis Tribune*'s Frank Force. With the score still tied, the teams battled into extra innings before the Senators pushed across a run in the twelfth for a 2–1 victory.

Off the field, another battle was brewing. According to the *Minneapolis Journal*'s report, as soon as the game was over the bleacher crowds broke through the fences, breaking locks of the gates and swarmed the field. Owens ran to the Columbus bench and took refuge under the stand. The crowd started throwing stones and clubs.

Captain Getchell and two or three policemen started to take Owens from the field. They were forced back into the bench and the crowd started hustling the officers away. Whenever an opening showed, stones or clubs were thrown at the umpire. Owens was badly scored but made no attempt to defend himself. He seemed content to let that duty fall upon the officials.

With the crowd growing larger and more unruly with each passing moment, one of the most prominent Minnesotans appeared and rescued Owens. As reported in the *Minneapolis Journal*, Walter W. "Pudge" Heffelfinger, an All-American football player at Yale and one of the greatest guards to ever play the game, "worked his way through to the bench, and, taking Owens by one arm started for the street with him. The stone throwing continued, altho [sic] there was a general recognition of 'Pudge' and a seeming reluctance to bounce any paving material off his head. It was not through any [fear] of 'Pudge's' muscular development, but more a reluctance to hit a popular man."

The six-foot-two, two-hundred-pound Heffelfinger—who in 1892 became the first professional football player when he was paid five hundred dollars by the Allegheny (Pennsylvania) Athletic Association to play against its rival, the Pittsburgh Athletic Club—hustled Owens to the Columbus bus, where he selected a relatively safe seat at the front. But once Heffelfinger left Owens, the rocks flew in such numbers that the driver could not take his

seat. According to the *Journal*, "Captain Getchell finally mounted the seat, and threatening to draw his revolver, lashed the horses out of the mob on to safety."

Two Columbus players were hit by rocks but not seriously injured. The *Journal* said the scene could have been worse: "Revolvers were in evidence throughout the crowd, but luckily no one fired a shot, as that was all that was needed to precipitate a dangerous melee."

The next day, nearly five thousand spectators—including one who stood outside the park and sold eggs to fans on their way in—gathered to see what would happen next. The *Journal* reported, "Minneapolis fandem was in a frenzy and the moment Owens appeared on the field, against the advice of police, a mighty jeer rose as from one throat."

After the first pitch, Owens was pelted with eggs, and he left the field claiming to be injured.

Minneapolis native Walter W. "Pudge" Heffelfinger, a three-time All-American at Yale, is considered one of the greatest linemen in college football history.

Several members of the 1905 Minneapolis Millers team, which finished third in the American Association, were involved in the 1906 controversy.

The game was ultimately forfeited to Columbus, which went on to win the final two games of the series, completing a four-game sweep and essentially ending the Millers' pennant hopes.

One week after the melee, the Millers filed a claim with the league office that Owens had bet on games. The previous month, Kelley had charged Owens with tipping signs to the opposing team, a claim he later withdrew. The league eventually cleared Owens of the charges, punishing Kelley for his false report by suspending him for the remainder of the season.

The Millers and their fans were demoralized. Attendance dwindled so much that the team's owner sold the franchise in August. The franchise was sold again following the season. And Kelley didn't return to the American Association until 1908. As for Heffelfinger, he who had gained notoriety from the violent sport of football earned lasting fame for his role as peacekeeper.

Harnessing a Record

Dan Patch Sets Pace at State Fair

Even a century ago, the right attraction could really draw a crowd to the Great Minnesota Get-Together. The main lures of the 1906 state fair were one of the most talented and well-known athletes of the day and the world record–breaking performance promised by his handlers—weather permitting, of course.

On September 8, 1906—a hot, still, late-summer day—a crowd estimated to number as many as ninety-three thousand gathered to watch Dan Patch, the top harness racer in the country, race against the clock. The horse, owned by Minneapolis businessman Marion W. Savage, would attempt to break his own world record for the mile: 1:55¼, set the previous year in Lexington, Kentucky. To promote the event, Savage and the horse's driver predicted in the Twin Cities' morning newspapers that Dan Patch would break the record if track conditions were favorable. That afternoon, the weather and the track both cooperated. The temperature reached the low nineties with little wind, and the track was in good condition.

According to George Barton, a Minneapolis sportswriter for fifty-four years, when Dan Patch and his driver, Harry Hersey, appeared on the track they were given a rousing ovation by the crowd, some of whom had come on special trains from Minnesota, Iowa, Nebraska, North Dakota, South Dakota, and Wisconsin. In his autobiography, *My Lifetime in Sports*, Barton said the rising crescendo became deafening as the starter waved his flag and Dan Patch, already in full stride, sped past the stand that housed the judges and timers. The spectators went wild at the announcement that the horse negotiated the first three-fourths mile in 1:29—an average of twenty-nine seconds per quarter-mile. The crowd knew that Dan Patch's last quarter-mile was always his fastest. He responded by covering the last quarter-mile in twenty-eight seconds for a new record of 1:55.

According to the next day's *Minneapolis Morning Tribune,* "the ovation accorded Dan Patch when the time was hung up was declared to be the greatest in the history of racing."

Dan Patch leads the pack in this circa 1900 race. The record he set at the 1906 Minnesota State Fair would not be broken until 1960.

The newspaper also reported that it took nearly fifty policemen to keep the crowd back from the track after the performance. But the cause of this vast celebration—the record, which was equaled in 1938 and stood until 1960—years later became a source of controversy.

Since 1902 Dan Patch had only run exhibitions against the clock, and on this day, as usual, he had a pacesetter ahead of him. The pace-setting sulky was equipped, as was common in trials against time, with a dust shield—a length of sailcloth stretched between the wheels—to protect Dan Patch from dirt and mud flying into his face.

Several years after his record-breaking feat, the governing body of harness racing legislated against this practice—calling the sailcloth a windshield—and eliminated Dan Patch's 1906 performance from the record books. But because Dan Patch was so well loved by the public and the press, the ruling was ignored and general record books of the day continued to list his feat.

Foaled in Indiana in 1896, Dan Patch didn't start racing until he was four, and he was purchased for sixty thousand dollars by Savage in 1902. Between 1900 and July 22, 1902—when he stopped racing against other pacers—Dan Patch was never beaten. From 1902 until he retired in 1909, he raced against the clock. Savage, a successful businessman who sold feed for farm animals through the International Stock Food Company, loved his horse, which had brought him wealth and fame. Dan Patch traveled to state fairs around the country in his own private railroad car. His earnings for Savage have been estimated as high as

$2 million. The horse, who set ten world records, was insured for one hundred twenty thousand dollars, while Savage reportedly had no life insurance.

After retiring in 1910, Dan Patch produced about one hundred off-spring. Barton wrote that during Dan Patch's retirement, tourists from all over the United States, Canada, Europe, and Australia made pilgrimages to the Savage farm to admire the horse. Barton also recalled an article in *Harness Horse,* a national magazine devoted to the equine world, that aptly described the public's love for Dan Patch: "men, women and children seemed content just to gaze upon Dan Patch in his stall as if he were George Washington or Abraham Lincoln." Barton described Patch as gentle and intelligent and endowed with personality. He recalled that, jogging down the track past the stands after an exhibition, Dan Patch had a way of nodding his head as if acknowledging the cheers.

On July 11, 1916, Dan Patch died at the age of twenty. Veterinarians said the death was due to an "athletic" heart induced by a slight sickness. The *Minneapolis Morning Tribune* reported that seventy-five of Dan Patch's performances averaged better than two minutes for the mile and "the strain of those efforts gave the horse an 'athletic heart,' which was the real cause of his death."

At the time of his horse's death, Savage was recovering from minor surgery in a Minneapolis hospital. His condition had been improving until he was informed of Dan Patch's passing. His doctors said the shock and grief he experienced were unbearable for him. Savage died the next day—thirty-two hours after his horse—of heart failure, at age fifty-seven.

Having never lost a competition, Dan Patch raced solely against the clock beginning in 1902.

First State Boys' Basketball Tournament Held

In early 1913, the faculty and athletic director of Carleton College in Northfield were looking for a way to showcase the school's newest building—Sayles-Hill Gymnasium. In March, a faculty committee announced its plan: a tournament to decide the state champion in boys' high school basketball. Each high school in the state was invited to submit its record.

The Carleton student newspaper reported: "The Committee met March 15 and went over the reports received. They were most gratifying. Over 20 schools sent in their certified records and others expressed approval."

The faculty committee and athletic director Claude J. Hunt planned to divide the state into eight regions and pick the team with the best regional record. But the committee found it difficult to eliminate schools because several regions had teams with nearly identical records. They eventually selected thirteen schools to compete for the first state championship—Austin, Blue Earth, Faribault, Fosston, Grand Rapids, Luverne, Madison, Mankato, Mountain Lake, Plainview, Red Wing, Stillwater, and Willmar—and announced that the tournament would be held during the first week of April.

According to the *Minneapolis Morning Tribune,* the college paid all expenses for six players and a coach for each team during the stay in Northfield and all railroad fares in excess of 150 miles so teams from distant parts of the state wouldn't be at a financial disadvantage.

On Thursday, April 3, the invitational tournament got under way with six games. In the opening game, Mountain Lake defeated Blue Earth 42–9. In the next game, Fosston, which had traveled the farthest, defeated Willmar 27–17. The other first-day results were Plainview over Austin, 29–20; Mankato over Faribault, 27–22; Luverne over Grand Rapids, 32–17; and Stillwater over Madison, 32–4.

On the tournament's second day, Fosston, Luverne, and Mountain Lake advanced to the

M.H.S. '10-11

MADISON H.S. STATE CHAMPIONS.

CHALMERS

Madison, which claimed the "mythical" state high school basketball championship in 1911, was one of thirteen teams that competed in the first "official" state tournament two years later.

semifinals with second-round victories. Then Luverne defeated Mankato 26–22, the latter hampered by the loss of one of its players to a knee injury suffered against Faribault the previous day. Fosston defeated Plainview 38–27 while Mountain Lake advanced with a 48–27 victory over Red Wing, which had a first-round bye. The fourth semifinalist was Stillwater, which received a second-round bye.

On Saturday morning, Fosston defeated Luverne 38–28 and Mountain Lake defeated Stillwater 31–24 to advance to the championship game, to be played later in the day.

That night, in front of two thousand enthusiastic fans, Fosston outlasted Mountain Lake

Sayles-Hill Gymnasium, on the Carleton College campus in Northfield, was the first home for the boys' state basketball tournament. Carleton played host to the tournament from 1913 to 1922.

29–27 to claim the first state title. The game was tied 16–16 at halftime. The *Minneapolis Journal* reported that the "Fosston players were the favorite of the entire three-day tournament because the members of the team were the smallest of any entered and because they showed more gameness and pluck." Likewise, the *Minneapolis Tribune* reported in its Monday edition, "Fosston had the smallest and lightest team of any at the tournament, averaging 130 pounds, yet their teamwork and rapid passing won in every game over their heavier opponents." The *Northfield Independent* agreed, saying Fosston's "performance is all the more wonderful when we consider the fact they did not even have a coach. They are to be complemented for their clean-cut and well-earned victory."

Incidentally, it was the only state title for Fosston, which would play in seven of the first nine state tournaments.

Starting the next year, congressional districts were used as the basis for selecting teams. Since not every congressional district had a qualified team, the number of teams varied from year to year, with as many as sixteen teams competing. Carleton College sponsored the tournament through 1916, when the Minnesota State High School Athletic Association was formed and took over the organization of high school activities in the state. Carleton continued to play host to the increasingly popular tournament for six more years. In 1923, the tournament moved to Kenwood Arena in Minneapolis to accommodate larger crowds. Just five years later, the tournament had outgrown Kenwood and relocated to the University of Minnesota campus.

DUESENBERG

A Race into the Record Books

St. Paul's Tommy Milton Wins Indianapolis 500

By the early 1920s, St. Paul's Tommy Milton was already one of the heroes of automobile racing. Milton, who started racing on county fair dirt tacks in Minnesota in 1913, gained national attention in 1917 when he defeated Barney Oldfield and several other well-known racers in a 100-mile national championship race. Three years later, Milton set a speed record—155 miles per hour—that would stand for six years.

But it was in Indianapolis that Milton's legacy took shape. In 1921, he won the Indianapolis 500. Just one of eight drivers to finish the race (out of a starting field of twenty-three), Milton averaged 89.62 miles per hour. Two years later, he became a racing legend. On Memorial Day 1923, in the eleventh running of the Indianapolis 500, the twenty-six-year-old Milton, who was legally blind in his right eye, became the first driver to win the Indianapolis 500 twice. Milton drove his midget eight-cylinder car—an H.C.S. Special—an average of 91.4 MPH before a record crowd of one hundred fifty thousand to claim the first-place prize of $28,500. Harry Hartz came in two laps (five minutes) behind Milton. Of the twenty-four cars that started the race, only eleven finished.

Milton overcame fatigue and severe blisters on his hands to win the race. The next day's *St. Paul Daily News* quoted Milton: "It's a great sensation to win the Indianapolis 500-mile race. It's a greater sensation to win it twice. I was greatly assisted by my teammate, Howdy Wilcox, who drove my car while I was having my blistered hands treated at the hospital." Milton had been leading the field for thirty-six laps when he made a pit stop in the 103rd lap for tires and supplies. Wilcox took over behind the wheel while Milton had his hands tended to. Wilcox drove for forty-eight laps; then Milton took over again in lap 151 and finished the 200-lap race.

"I was tired at the finish, but victory assuaged the severe blisters on my hands and the natural fatigue of such a long grind," Milton reported to the *St. Paul Daily News.* "I believe I

In 1923, St. Paul's Tommy Milton, who was legally blind in his right eye, became the first driver to win the Indianapolis 500 twice.

was more fatigued at the end of the 500-mile race in 1921. My motor never missed a shot."

Milton retired from competitive auto racing in 1931. At one time, he held fifty racing titles. In 104 career starts, Milton won twenty-three races and finished in the top three eighty-two times. On May 5, 1958, the Minnesota Sports Hall of Fame was unveiled with an inaugural class of seventeen inductees—Milton among them. Reporter Tom Briere commented on the ceremony in the next day's *Minneapolis Tribune:* "Tommy Milton, acclaimed the greatest race car driver of all time, was so blind in one eye he couldn't pass the road test, [Milton said] 'but I got into it because I didn't know any better.'"

September 19, 1926
29 Football Games in 117 Days

Duluth Eskimos
Barnstorm for the NFL

The Duluth Eskimos weren't much of a factor in the chase for the 1926 National Football League title. Three teams—the Frankford (Pennsylvania) Yellowjackets (14–1–2), Chicago Bears (12–1–3), and Pottsville (Pennsylvania) Maroons (10–2–2)—were the class of the league. The Eskimos compiled an ordinary 6–5–3 record and finished in eighth place among the league's twenty-two teams. Despite this mediocre standing, the 1926 Eskimos became an NFL legend and, according to some league historians, may have saved the NFL.

The NFL was struggling financially in its fifth season. The league's teams—primarily based in the East and Midwest—were hampered by months of poor weather that greatly affected attendance. The league also faced a serious challenge from the upstart American Football League, which was competing head-to-head against the NFL in at least four cities.

The league got a much-needed boost from the Eskimos, owned by Ole Haugsrud, who had assumed control of the struggling franchise three years earlier. To ease the team's financial situation, Haugsrud enlisted the services of one of his high school friends—Superior (Wisconsin) Central schoolmate Ernie Nevers, who at Stanford had became one of the greatest college football players of all time. Born in Willow River, Minnesota, Nevers was also one of the greatest all-around college athletes, earning eleven letters in four sports in just three years.

In summer 1926, Nevers was playing professional baseball for the St. Louis Browns of the American League. In August, Haugsrud offered his friend the incredible sum of fifteen thousand dollars plus a percentage of gate receipts to play for the Eskimos. After Nevers agreed, Haugsrud promoted the team as "Ernie Nevers' Eskimos."

Ernie Nevers, a Willow River native, played major league baseball and professional football after attending Stanford University.

In early September, the twenty-four-year-old Nevers left the Browns and joined the Eskimos—whose roster included future Pro Football Hall of Famers Walt Kiesling and Johnny "Blood" McNally—in Two Harbors for training camp. After a week of practice, the Eskimos played an exhibition game on September 12 against the Gogebic (Michigan) Panthers at

Superior's Hislop Park. The Eskimos won 25–0 to the cheers of three thousand fans.

The Eskimos' legend was launched the following Sunday, when they opened league play with a home game against the Kansas City Cowboys. In front of a crowd of six thousand, the Eskimos pulled out a 7–0 victory. The only touchdown was a fumble recovery and short return by Jack Underwood. Nevers kicked the extra point. The game was the only home game for the Eskimos, as the team's fifteen players went on a 25-game, 117-day barnstorming tour. The Eskimos did not return home until February 5.

In addition to the thirteen league games, the Eskimos played exhibitions in most of the NFL cities and on the West Coast. In one eight-day stretch, the Eskimos competed in five games. During the tour, Nevers rarely left the field, reportedly missing just twenty-seven minutes of action the entire season.

The Eskimos went 14–8–3 on the tour, and Grantland Rice, the dean of twentieth-century American sportswriters, dubbed them "The Iron Men from the North." The *Football Encyclopedia*

Halfback Walter Gayer, from Creighton University, evades a tackle during training camp for the Duluth Eskimos, who, along with Ernie Nevers, are credited with rescuing the NFL in 1926.

recapped the 1926 season, noting, "Nevers gave the NFL a needed heroic image and some gate pull in a season of rain and red ink." Following the season, the *Green Bay Press Gazette* named Nevers the fullback on the all-NFL team.

The next season, the fortunes of both the Eskimos and the NFL declined. Ten of the league's twenty-two teams folded prior to the season, and the Eskimos followed suit after playing all of their games on the road and compiling a 1–8 record. Nevers, who continued to play baseball in 1927 and 1928, went on to play football for the Chicago Cardinals. In 1929, he set an NFL record that still stands, scoring 40 points (six touchdowns and four extra points) in a game against the Chicago Bears. He retired in 1932.

Nevers and Haugsrud were crucial in helping the NFL survive its infancy. After selling the dormant Eskimos franchise in 1929, Haugsrud received a promise from the NFL that if a franchise was ever granted in Minnesota again he would have the first option to buy. In 1960, Haugsrud was part of the original Minnesota Vikings ownership group. In 1976, the former high school teammates passed away six weeks apart.

Bronko Nagurski (center) scored the only touchdown in the Gophers' 6–0 victory over the Badgers in Madison, Wisconsin, in 1928.

November 24, 1928
Football's First "Iron Man"

Bronko Nagurski Leads Gophers over Badgers

A member of both the College and Pro Football Halls of Fame, Bronko Nagurski played three seasons of football for the University of Minnesota before embarking on two separate professional athletic careers, in football and wrestling. In his days on the field and more than a dozen years in the ring, Nagurski gave a lot of memorable performances. But in 1958, when he was named to the Minnesota Sports Hall of Fame, he easily selected one game as the most unforgettable of his career, telling the *Minneapolis Star*, "There is no use in my trying to dig up a new 'greatest thrill.' Mine always will be that Wisconsin game at Madison in 1928 . . ."

Charles Johnson, long-time sports editor of the *Minneapolis Star* and the *Minneapolis Tribune*, wrote in 1958 that Nagurski's performance against the Badgers in 1928 "is still regarded as one of the greatest all-around efforts in Big Ten history." In that final game of the 1928 season, Nagurski added new meaning to the phrase "playing hurt."

Nagurski had joined the Gopher varsity the previous year as a sophomore and helped the team to an undefeated season. The Gophers went 6–0–2 overall (one of those games—a 7–7 tie against Notre Dame—is considered another of Nagurski's greatest performances) and 3–0–1 in the Big Ten to earn a share of the conference title. They opened the 1928 season with three consecutive victories, fueling thoughts of another conference title. The fourth game of the Gophers' season was against the Iowa Hawkeyes in Iowa City.

The Gophers were clinging to a 6–0 lead in the fourth quarter when the Hawkeyes rallied for a 7–6 victory. Ruining the Gophers' hopes of a conference title, the loss was even

more costly because Nagurski was hurt late in the game. The *Minneapolis Tribune* reported that Nagurski's injury—two fractured ribs—was expected to keep him out of the lineup at least two weeks. But the following Saturday, in Evanston, Illinois, Nagurski joined the offensive line as the Gophers took on Northwestern.

The Wildcats handed the Gophers their second consecutive one-point loss—this time 10–9. Again the defeat was doubly painful as another starter, George Gibson—who would be named an All-American following the season—fractured his shoulder. The *Minneapolis Tribune*'s George Barton reported that Nagurski "played superbly on the line in spite of the handicap under which he worked due to his fractured ribs and injured spine."

The Gophers rebounded with victories over Indiana, 21–12, and the Haskell Indians, 52–0, to take a 5–2 record into the season finale against Wisconsin. The Badgers, who brought a 7–0–1 record into the game, were confident they would complete an undefeated season—earning their first conference title since 1912—with a victory over the banged-up Gophers.

At least five thousand Gopher fans journeyed to Madison—many on sixteen Great Northern "special" trains—to see if their team could derail the Badgers' title hopes. The Gophers went into the game as underdogs for the first time in three seasons, but coach Clarence Spears gave the Gopher faithful reason to be optimistic when he announced that Gibson would play and that Nagurski would return to his fullback position. Nagurski, who wore a steel corset to protect his ribs and spine (the injury was later described as two broken vertebrae), rose to the occasion.

Early in the second quarter, Nagurski recovered a fumble at the Badgers' 17-yard line, and five plays later he scored a touchdown to give the Gophers a 6–0 lead. In the third quarter, he prevented a game-tying touchdown when he caught Badgers quarterback Bo Cuisinier from behind at the Gophers' 10-yard line. Moments later, when the Badgers went for a touchdown on fourth down, Nagurski knocked down Cuisinier's pass. The Gophers held on for a 6–0 victory.

The headlines in the *Minneapolis Tribune* the next day summed up Nagurski's performance: "Nagurski recovers fumble and batters way to touchdown. . . . Bronko rises to greatest heights of his career." Barton wrote, "the names of Nagurski, Arthur Pharmer and Fred Hovde will live long in the memory of Minnesota rooters."

The memory of the victory never faded for Nagurski. "They were the favorites, of course," Nagurski recalled for the *Minneapolis Star* thirty years later, "and we were pretty well battered up. We had a lot of trouble keeping them from scoring, but we did and after all these years, I can think of no game that gives me more satisfaction."

In 1929, Nagurski was named a first-team All-American at two positions—defensive line and fullback. He remains the only player to be named All-American at two positions in the same season. The next year, Nagurski joined the Chicago Bears. He retired following the 1937 season but returned to the Bears for a final season in 1943. In December 1999—nine

Bronko Nagurski, the only college football player to be named an All-American at two positions in the same year, earned fame as a professional football player and wrestler.

years after his death — *Sports Illustrated* named Nagurski Minnesota's top athlete of the twentieth century, and his name lives on in the Bronko Nagurski Trophy, awarded yearly to college football's best defensive player by the Football Writers Association of America and the Charlotte Touchdown Club.

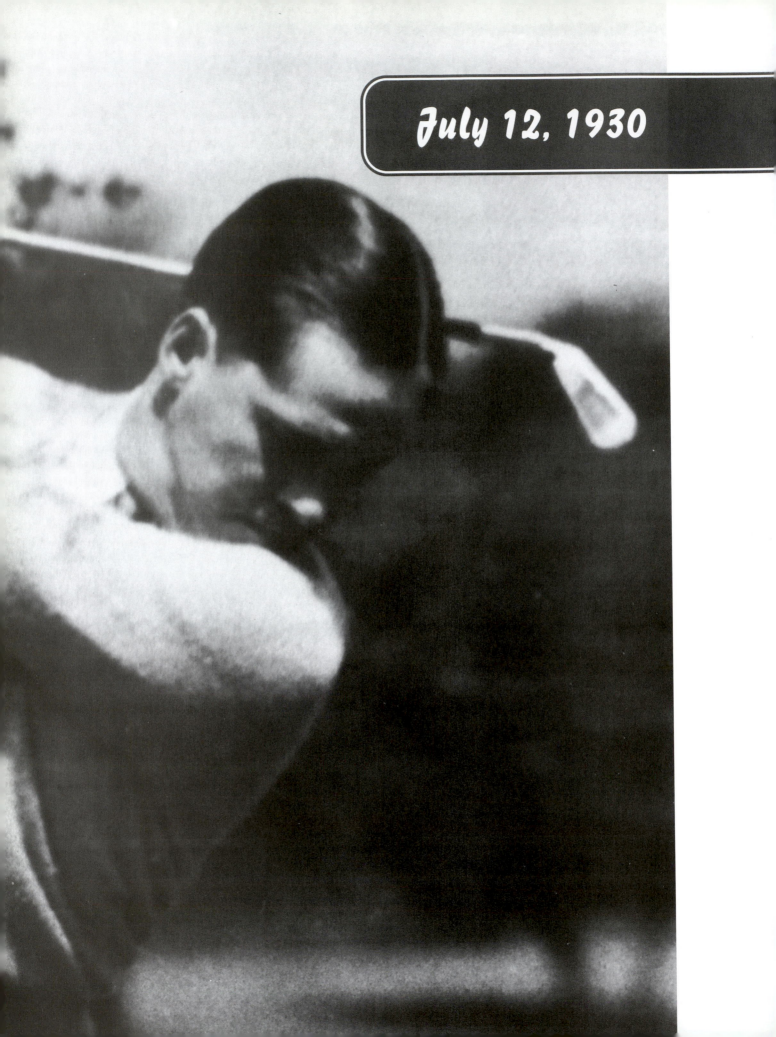

July 12, 1930

Jones Scorches Interlachen

Bobby Jones Victorious at U.S. Open

Jn early July 1930, hot weather settled over Minneapolis with high temperatures in the nineties. During the heat wave, a golfer from Atlanta, Georgia, came to town riding a personal hot streak.

Bobby Jones's streak had actually started in 1923. Between 1923 and 1929, Jones won nine major golf titles. Even better, in 1930 Jones became just the third American to win the British Amateur, which had been played since 1885, and he also won the British Open for the third time. Jones arrived in Minneapolis looking for his third major title of the year. The 72-hole U.S. Open would be played at Interlachen Country Club over two days.

After the first two rounds, Jones trailed the leader, Horton Smith, by two strokes. Smith had shot 72 and 70 while Jones had recorded 71 and 73. Smith's lead vanished in the third round, however, when Jones shot a four-under-par 68 while Smith scored a 76. After this round, dubbed one of golf's greatest exhibitions by Grantland Rice, the country's foremost golf writer, Jones took a five-stroke lead going into the final.

But in that round Jones's lead gradually disappeared with three uncharacteristic double bogeys. The third one—on the seventeenth hole—left him with a one-stroke lead over Mac-Donald Smith, who had started the final round seven strokes behind Jones. But Jones recovered on the par-four, 402-yard eighteenth hole: he sank an uphill 40-foot putt for a birdie, sending the fifteen thousand spectators into a frenzy. Smith, needing an eagle to tie, parred number eighteen to finish two strokes behind the leader. Jones's score of 287 was just one stroke shy of the 72-hole record set fourteen years earlier by Chicago's Chick Evans as he won the National Open at Minikahda.

In the next day's *Minneapolis Tribune*, Rice reported, "Bobby Jones broke all records in the history of golf Saturday afternoon by winning his third major championship in succession, and this is a matter of historical data that goes back 500 years. This is a plain statement of fact that no adjective can adorn."

Bobby Jones, five-time winner of the U.S. Amateur Golf Championship, earned his third major championship of 1930 by dominating the U.S. Open at Interlachen Country Club.

Jones continued his hot streak when he won the U.S. Amateur in September in Philadelphia. It was the fifth U.S. Amateur title for Jones, who had previously won the tournament in 1924, 1925, 1927, and 1928. (Minnesotan Harrison "Jimmy" Johnston won the tournament in 1929.) After winning at Interlachen in July, Jones hinted that he might retire following the U.S. Amateur, and after completing the Grand Slam, he did. Jones's legacy lives on in the Master's Tournament, which he helped create in 1931.

September 4, 1933
"Unser Choe"

Millers' Hauser Hits Sixtieth Home Run

Baseball fans can be hard on an opposing team's players, and in a local rivalry like the one between the Minneapolis Millers and the St. Paul Saints, fans can be relentless. In the early 1930s, Saints fans directed a lot of verbal abuse at the Millers' Joe Hauser.

Hauser, who hit seventy-nine home runs in six major-league seasons in the 1920s, astounded baseball fans in 1930. That season, he hit sixty-three home runs—a professional baseball record—while playing for the Baltimore Orioles of the International League. After joining the Millers in 1932, Hauser continued to hit, leading the American Association with forty-nine home runs. But Saints fans were unimpressed by Hauser's home-run totals, arguing that he benefited from playing at Nicollet Park, where the dimensions—279 feet down the right field line—greatly favored a left-handed hitter like Hauser.

The thirty-four-year-old Hauser unintentionally reinforced this argument at the start of the 1933 season. The winner of three consecutive home-run titles went homerless in the Millers' first nine games, which were all played on the road. Hauser, who was called *Unser Choe* (German for "Our Joe") by Millers fans, hit his first home run of the season in the Millers' home opener on April 27.

But even the most skeptical fans should have been impressed by Hauser's performance as the season continued to unfold. Once he started hitting home runs, American Association pitchers seldom shut him out. By the end of June, the five-foot-ten, 175-pound Hauser had thirty-two home runs. After homering in seven consecutive games in mid-July, he had forty-one. He hit his fiftieth in game 105, and on August 13 he broke the American Association record of fifty-four (set by the Millers' Nick Cullop in 1930) with his fifty-fifth home run.

Joe Hauser hit his sixty-third and sixty-fourth home runs of the 1933 season at St. Paul's Lexington Park on September 4.

A week later, Hauser connected in the Millers' 134th game to become the first player in professional baseball history to twice hit at least sixty home runs in a season. Having reached that plateau with three weeks remaining in the regular season, Hauser set his sights on his personal best of sixty-three, which had surpassed Babe Ruth's major-league standard of sixty-one, hit in 1927. But he cooled off momentarily—hitting just two home runs over the next two weeks—leaving him one shy of the record going into the Millers' Labor Day double-header against the Saints.

Holiday double-headers—a game at each ballpark—were a tradition for the Millers and the Saints. The first game of the day was played at Lexington Park in St. Paul. The spacious Lexington Park was the antithesis of cozy Nicollet Park: Lexington's right-field fence was 365 feet from home plate with a thirty-foot wall at the top of a ten-foot embankment.

On an overcast, windy, dreary morning, Hauser went hitless in his first three at bats (walking in one of them), his performance fueling the critical Saints fans. After a rain delay of nearly thirty minutes in the fourth inning, Hauser came to the plate with the Millers clinging to a 3–2 lead. Hauser connected and watched as the baseball was nearly blown foul by the wind before it cleared the right-field fence, fair by inches.

In his next at bat, Hauser silenced the yells of "lucky stiff" with another gigantic drive, which Gordon Gilmore of the *St. Paul Pioneer Press* reported "appeared to land on top of the right-field fence and then bounce over, fair by many yards." He added, "incidentally, it was the first time that anyone has hit two home runs over Lexington's long right-field barrier in the same game."

The two home runs—the sixty-third and sixty-fourth for Hauser—helped the Millers hold on for a 5–3 victory. In the afternoon game at Nicollet Park, Hauser added another home run, clearing the left-center field wall by thirty feet. The *Minneapolis Star*'s Charles Johnson noted, "it was a dramatic way for this powerful slugger to break the record. It has been in St. Paul where Joe had to take the most bitter jibe from the fans. 'Home run at Nicollet' has been the cry from the downriver customers every time Joe got the ball into the air at Lexington. And to think he would choose that large enclosure to equal and break his mighty record must have given him the greatest thrill of his career."

But Hauser didn't rest on his laurels. He hit four more home runs to increase his total to sixty-nine, the last two in the Millers' 8–6 loss to the Kansas City Blues on the next-to-last day of the season. After hitting seven home runs in the final week of the regular season, he missed a chance at number seventy when the Millers' final game was canceled because of wet grounds.

The next season, Hauser picked up where he left off, hitting seventeen home runs and driving in forty in the Millers' first twenty games. It looked like he would challenge the record. Even after missing three weeks in June with a knee injury, he kept hitting home runs. He

Joe Hauser became the first player in professional baseball history to twice hit at least sixty home runs in a season when he belted sixty-nine homers for the Minneapolis Millers in 1933.

had thirty-three in the Millers' first eighty-two games before suffering a fractured kneecap in a game against Kansas City on July 29. The injury forced him to miss the rest of the season.

Hauser returned for two more years with the Millers—hitting twenty-three and thirty-four home runs—before retiring after the 1936 season. He came out of retirement to play for Sheboygan of the Wisconsin State League from 1940 to 1942. Hauser, whose plaque at the Wisconsin Athletic Hall of Fame gives him the title "home-run king of the minors," died in 1997 at the age of ninety-eight.

Entering a Golden Era

Gophers Defeat Pitt en route to National Title

Though Minnesota was first dubbed the Gopher State in 1858, the adjective "Golden" wasn't always a part of the nickname for University of Minnesota athletic teams. Legendary sportswriter and radio announcer Halsey Hall first called the Gophers "Golden" in the 1930s because of their yellow football jerseys and pants. Fittingly, around the same time the Gopher football team entered a "golden" era.

The Gophers won or shared eight conference football titles between 1903 and 1927, but it was Bernie Bierman's arrival in 1932 that ushered the program into the national spotlight. In his second season, Bierman directed the Gophers to a 4–0–4 record and a share of the conference title—their first in six seasons. The highlight of the 1933 season was the Gophers' 7–3 victory at home over Pittsburgh, considered one of the top teams in the East.

With both teams expected to be strong again in 1934, the rematch—in Pittsburgh—was eagerly anticipated. Most college football experts were calling it the game of the year, predicting that the winner would be the frontrunner for the national championship. In a preview story, *Minneapolis Tribune* sports editor George Barton wrote, "the game has stirred up such widespread interest that 60,000 spectators are expected to witness the struggle, which will be broadcast over a national hook-up and covered by the leading football writers of New York, Philadelphia, Boston, Cleveland, Detroit and Chicago." In fact, many of the experts were going to see the Gophers in person for the first time. Prior to the 1934 season, the farthest east the Gopher football team had been was Columbus, Ohio.

The Gophers and Pittsburgh built the anticipation when they each opened the season with two victories. The Gophers beat North Dakota State 56–12 and Nebraska 20–0 to run their unbeaten streak to ten games, while Pittsburgh defeated West Virginia 27–6 and Southern California 20–6.

In his syndicated weekly column, sportswriter Grantland Rice picked the Gophers to

Bernie Bierman coached the Gopher football team to five national championships, the first in 1934.

win "in a hammering, battering, low-scoring jamboree." But the Gophers didn't live up to these expectations in the first half of that afternoon's contest, as the Panthers outplayed them to take a 7–0 lead at the intermission. Barton reported in the next day's *Tribune* that at halftime he and the Gophers were subjected to much ridicule by members of the press: "So that's the great Minnesota team we've been hearing so much about, eh? Why, they are just a bunch of mugs who think they can play football. Where's all those powerhouse and deception plays we've read about?"

The Gophers answered those questions in the second half. Still trailing 7–0 after three quarters, they finally tied the game early in the final quarter on a 22-yard touchdown run by Julius Alfonse and an extra-point kick by Bill Bevan. After forcing the Panthers to punt on their ensuing possession, the Gophers quickly marched inside the Panthers' 20-yard line. From there, the Gophers used a little deception to score the go-ahead touchdown.

On a fourth down, Stan Kostka took the snap from center, and as he headed into the line he handed off to Glenn Seidel, who lateraled to halfback Pug Lund. Lund ran wide and then threw a pass to Bob Tenner, who caught the ball at the 7-yard line and went in for a touchdown. The stunned Panthers didn't recover as the Gophers held on for a 13–7 victory. Years later, Bierman recalled the play for the *Minneapolis Star:* "It's hard to pick out any one play or incident over so many years. But I guess I'd still take the winning touchdown [against Pittsburgh]. The play that scored was a variation off the buck lateral series, and we'd never used it before in a game."

Barton wrote on the front page of the next day's *Sunday Tribune,* "It calls for rare courage and almost superhuman endurance to stage the comeback the Gophers showed. Football critics and rooters of the East have read and heard much about Minnesota's offensive play over a period of years. Saturday they gained convincing proof that the Gophers are everything that had been said of them."

The following Saturday, the Gophers routed Iowa 48–12 in Iowa City. In November, they defeated Michigan 34–0, Indiana 30–0, and Chicago 35–7 before completing their unblemished season with a 34–0 victory at Wisconsin. Following the season, the Gophers were awarded their first national championship, having outscored their eight opponents 270–38. They went on to win national titles in each of the next two seasons and added national titles in 1940 and 1941.

The decade between 1932 and 1941 was truly "golden" for the Gophers. In that ten-season span, they won seven conference titles and five national titles while going undefeated five times. At the end of the decade, the Gophers were 63–12–5 and had lost only eight conference games. In his autobiography, Barton, who covered University of Minnesota football for over fifty years, called the 1934 team the best Gopher team of all time and the 1934 contest between the Gophers and the Panthers the "top contest" he had ever seen.

Halfback Pug Lund was a key member of the Gophers' first national football championship team. The All-American completed a pass to Bob Tenner for the game-winning touchdown in the Gophers' 13–7 come-from-behind victory over Pittsburgh in 1934.

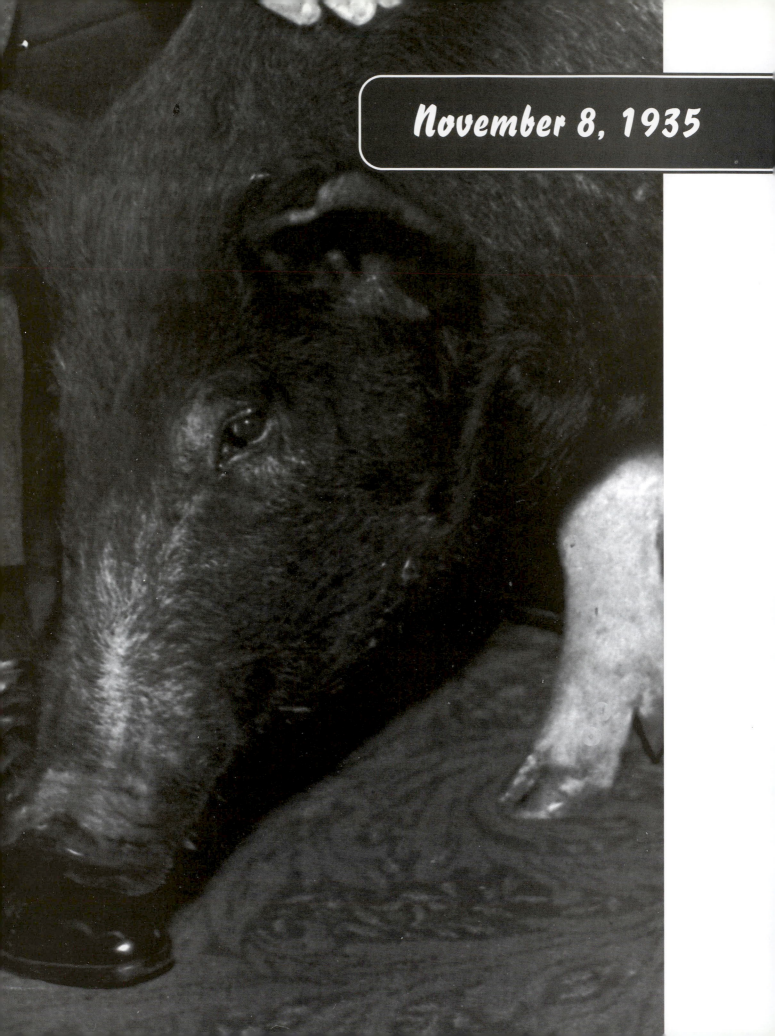

Floyd of Rosedale

Gophers Conquer Hawkeyes, Claim Pig as Trophy

Emotions always run high when Minnesota and Iowa football teams meet, but the pregame hype in 1935 reached new levels. Out of the rhetoric, one of the most famous trophies in college football was created.

In 1934, the Gophers dominated Iowa 48–12 en route to an undefeated season and the school's first national championship. After that game several Iowa newspapers accused the Gophers of intentionally trying to harm Oz Simmons, the Hawkeyes' star running back, who had been forced to leave the game because of an injury.

The controversy was rekindled by an unlikely source before the teams' rematch in 1935. The night before the game, Iowa governor Clyde Herring told an *Associated Press* reporter in Des Moines, "The University of Iowa football team will defeat the University of Minnesota tomorrow. Those Minnesotans will find 10 other top-notch football players besides Oz Simmons against them this year. Moreover, if the officials stand for any rough tactics like Minnesota used last year, I'm sure the crowd won't."

Herring's statement ran in newspapers nationwide, drawing immediate reaction from the Gophers' traveling party. "I cannot understand a governor making such a statement," Gopher coach Bernie Bierman told the *Minneapolis Tribune*. Bierman thought Herring's comments were inflammatory and encouraged the Hawkeyes crowd to take charge if they thought their team wasn't being treated fairly. He also asked for extra police protection for his team and threatened that if the crowd's behavior toward the Gophers was unruly in any fashion it would be the end of athletic relations between the two schools. The parents of some Gopher football players asked Minnesota governor Floyd B. Olson to mobilize the National Guard to protect them.

Olson elected to use diplomacy and tact to defuse the situation. Just hours before the game, Olson sent Herring a telegram:

"Floyd of Rosedale" is awarded annually to the winner of the Minnesota-Iowa football game.

Dear Clyde: Minnesota folks excited over your statement about the Iowa crowd lynching the Minnesota football team. I have assured them that you are a law-abiding gentleman and are only trying to get our goat. The Minnesota team will tackle clean, but oh, how hard, Clyde. If you seriously think Iowa has any chance to win, I will bet you a Minnesota prize hog that Minnesota wins today. The loser must deliver the hog to the winner in person. You are getting odds because Minnesota raises better hogs than Iowa. My best personal regards and condolences. Floyd B. Olson, Governor of Minnesota.

Governor Herring didn't have time to respond to Olson's telegram but told an *Associated Press* reporter in Iowa City that the governors had a bet.

The game was played without incident other than one roughing penalty against the Gophers, which drew a chorus of boos from the Iowa fans. The Hawkeyes limited the Gophers, who had averaged 26 points per game in their first five games, to just four first downs in the first half and led 7–0 at halftime. But the Gophers silenced the crowd of fifty thousand by dominating the second half, restricting the Hawkeyes to just one first down after the intermission as they rallied for a 13–7 victory.

After the game, Herring told the *Minneapolis Tribune* that his comments from the previ-

ous day had been misconstrued and added, "Yes, sir, instead of getting their goat, I lost a pig. Floyd said he'd bet me a prize Minnesota pig against a prized Iowa pig. But he's used to those scrawny pigs they have in Minnesota and I'm going to find a razorback so it won't hurt his digestion. I'm going to take the pig to St. Paul in a truck and personally herd it into Olson's office. I hope his carpet wears well. The pig will be named either Floyd or Floydina depending on the sex."

A few days later Herring delivered "Floyd," a pig donated by Rosedale Farms of Fort Dodge, Iowa, to Olson's office. Floyd's likeness was sculpted into a bronze statue fifteen inches high and twenty-one inches long. Every year since 1935, the rivals have competed for "Floyd." The Gophers lead the all-time series with the Hawkeyes 58–36 with two ties.

Minnesota governor Floyd B. Olson and Iowa governor Clyde Herring wagered a hog over the outcome of the Minnesota-Iowa football game in 1935.

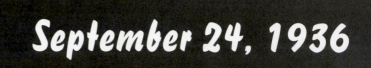

September 24, 1936

Coach Bernie Bierman and university cop Herman Glander board a train bound for Seattle, Washington. The Gopher football party was in for an eventful trip.

A Harrowing Road Trip

Gophers Escape Hotel Fire in Missoula, Montana

*J*n 1936, playing a game outside of the Midwest was still a rarity for the University of Minnesota football team. Only twice had the Gophers ventured beyond the region's borders—in 1931, to Palo Alto, California, to play Stanford, and in 1934, to Pittsburgh [see pages 50–53].

But after opening the previous four seasons against either South Dakota State or North Dakota State, Gopher coach Bernie Bierman was looking for a tougher opponent for the Gophers' season opener. Bierman decided his two-time defending national champions, riding a 24-game unbeaten streak, would open their season against the University of Washington in Seattle.

On Tuesday, September 22, the Gophers boarded their special Pullman train in Minneapolis for the four-day trip to the Pacific Northwest. Their itinerary included a stop in Miles City, Montana, for practice and an overnight stay in Missoula, Montana, at the Florence Hotel. According to *Minneapolis Tribune* sports editor George Barton, if it weren't for a light-sleeping newspaperman, the Gophers' trip might have ended in Missoula.

Barton reported on the eventful night in the September 25 edition of the *Tribune*. Early in the morning of September 24, several hours after retiring for the night, Edward L. Shave, veteran sports editor for the *St. Paul Daily News,* was awakened in his hotel room by the smell of smoke. At first he thought the odor was from nearby forest fires, but it became so strong that Shave opened the door of his room to investigate and discovered the corridor filled with smoke.

Shave dashed downstairs and told an employee that the hotel was on fire. While Shave ran outside to ring a fire alarm, the employee telephoned Bierman's room. Bierman, his assistants, and three student managers roused the players. Some of Gophers thought it was a practical joke, but eventually all of them were convinced of the fire. The team members,

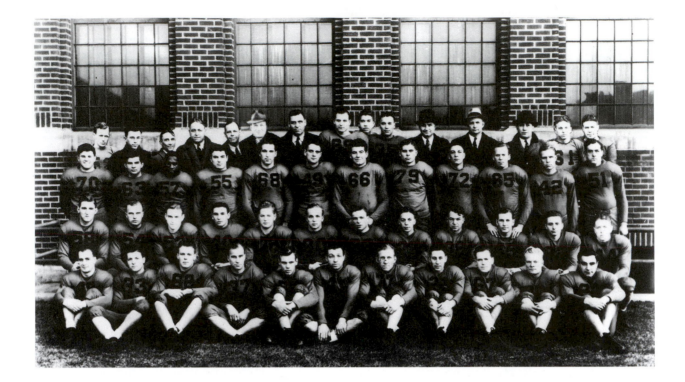

The 1936 University of Minnesota football team survived a scare in Missoula, Montana, before winning its third consecutive national championship.

many of them dressed in their pajamas, gathered in the lobby and were quickly ushered to the railroad station, where they boarded their train. Ninety minutes later, the entire building was engulfed in flames, and when the players returned around 9 A.M. to claim their belongings, it was too late.

Firefighters had been unable to control the blaze, and the four-story building was completely gutted. By 11 A.M. just three walls remained, and they were soon pulled down by Missoula firemen. The fire, which started in the basement of a drug store in the building, reportedly by spontaneous combustion, did an estimated five hundred thousand dollars in property damage. Barton calculated that the Minnesota party lost personal belongings valued at two thousand dollars and about twenty-five hundred dollars worth of team equipment.

George Edmond reported in the *St. Paul Pioneer Press*, "hardly a Gopher escaped without some loss in the fire. Many of them lost their shoes but they were taken to Missoula stores and re-outfitted." Barton wrote for the *Tribune*, "but for Shave's prompt action, many of the players might have lost their lives as the fire got underway most rapidly in the section of the hotel where they were quartered. This portion collapsed less than two hours after the fire started."

In his column the next day, Shave took no credit for discovering the fire. The *St. Paul Daily News* ran two photographs—one of the hotel with just its walls standing and the other of one of the Gopher football players who had been partially overcome by smoke. The player was being helped by Herman Glander, the University's "campus cop," who was making his first football trip in twenty-eight years. The caption to the picture of the hotel said, "all occupants escaped uninjured when roused by Ed L. Shave, who had discovered the fire."

The fire apparently had no adverse effect on the team. The Gophers held a productive practice at the University of Montana in Missoula that afternoon before resuming their trip to Seattle. A crowd of forty thousand warmly greeted them in Seattle. Washington coach Jimmy Phelan told the *Associated Press*: "I'm sorry to hear of the plight of coach Bernie Bierman and his men. I hope the fire didn't cause any ill effects. We want the Gophers to be at full strength."

Through three quarters, the teams played to a 7–7 tie, but a fourth quarter touchdown pass from Andy Uram to Ray King helped the Gophers pull out a 14–7 victory. Future coaching legend Bud Wilkinson caught a crucial 60-yard pass for the Gophers while teammate Julius Alfonse intercepted three Huskie passes.

Having survived a bigger test than Bierman expected, the Gophers returned home to defeat Nebraska the following week. They then beat Michigan and Purdue to stretch their unbeaten streak to 28 games before they were stunned by Northwestern, 6–0, in Evanston, Illinois, on October 31. The Gophers regrouped and closed out the season with three consecutive impressive victories—over Iowa 52–0, Texas 47–19, and Wisconsin 24–0. And, despite not winning the conference title, they were named the national champion for the third consecutive season. With a 7–1 record, the Gophers had outscored their opponents 203–32.

November 15, 1941

Bruce Smith to the Rescue

Halfback Keys Gopher Victory Against Iowa

In the next-to-last game of the 1941 season, the Gopher football team was struggling against the Iowa Hawkeyes in Iowa City. The defending national champions went into the November 15 game sporting a 15-game unbeaten streak, but they lacked one of their best players—halfback Bruce Smith. The loss of Smith, a senior from Faribault, was significant.

Smith had scored the game-winning touchdown in three come-from-behind victories in the Gophers' unbeaten season in 1940 and had scored two touchdowns in their 14–6 victory at Washington in the 1941 season opener. After playing sparingly in the Gophers' next two games (victories over Pittsburgh and Illinois), Smith keyed their 7–0 victory over Michigan. With the game tied 0–0 in the second quarter, Smith completed a 43-yard pass to Herman Frickey, giving the Gophers a first down at the 5-yard line. Three plays later, Frickey scored on a two-yard run and Bill Garnaas kicked the extra point to make it 7–0. The Gophers played the second half without Smith, who was injured on the play following the completion. Smith was re-injured the following week in the Gophers' 8–7 victory over Northwestern and sat out their 9–0 victory over Nebraska.

Without Smith in the lineup against Iowa, the Hawkeyes thought they could contain the Gophers by putting eight defenders on the line of scrimmage. Their strategy worked early in the game, as the Hawkeyes, who brought a 3–3 record into the game but had lost nine of the previous ten meetings between the two teams, took advantage of Smith's absence to seize a 7–0 lead.

Midway through the first quarter, with the Gophers' offense misfiring, coach Bernie Bierman knew his team needed a spark. Having proven himself on many occasions over the previous two seasons, Smith was just the one to provide it. When he dashed onto the field late in the first quarter, the six thousand Minnesota fans among the crowd of 43,200 roared

Bruce Smith is the only Gopher to earn the Heisman Trophy, awarded annually to the nation's top college football player.

their approval. Smith immediately made an impact—with his arm. On his first play, Smith completed a 39-yard pass to Garnaas. Moments later he completed a nine-yard pass to Garnaas, setting up Bill Daley's three-yard touchdown run. The Gophers repossessed the ball and went on a 93-yard scoring drive to take a 13–6 lead. The crucial play of the drive was Smith's 31-yard run, which got the Gophers out of a hole from their 8-yard line.

After the Gophers missed the extra point, the Hawkeyes answered with a touchdown to tie the game 13–13. But that was it for the Hawkeyes, as the Gophers scored again before halftime to take a 20–13 lead at the intermission. The Gophers added two touchdowns in the fourth quarter to earn a 34–13 victory. After managing just two first downs in the first quarter without Smith, they finished with 24. Smith, who rushed for 52 yards in nine carries, also passed for 74 yards. Charles Johnson reported in the *Minneapolis Star Journal,* "If Bruce's exhibition today of real stuff in the pinch didn't make him All-American, we say toss the pickers into the ashcan."

Having survived the Hawkeyes' challenge, the Gophers completed a second consecutive undefeated season with a 41–6 victory over Wisconsin. The headline in the *Minneapolis Star*

Journal summed up that performance: "Gophers tip Badgers, 41–6, win Big Ten, U.S. titles. Smith heroic in last game." Johnson reported that Smith "closed out his spectacular career with his greatest of many outstanding performances." Smith rushed for 88 yards—including runs of 42 and 39 yards—completed three passes for 90 yards, and also intercepted a pass. Recapping the national championship season—the Gophers' fifth in eight years—Bierman wrote in the *Star Journal* that the pass Smith completed in the Michigan game was the team's "best-executed play of the season."

Shortly following the season, Smith was honored as the winner of the Heisman Trophy, awarded annually to the nation's top college football player. Smith, the Gophers' third-leading rusher in 1941, is the only Gopher to ever win the award, outpolling Notre Dame's Angelo Bertelli and Stanford's Frankie Albert. Accompanied by his father, Lucius, who had played for the Gophers in 1910 and 1911, and sister, Olive, Smith received the award at a banquet in New York City on December 9, 1941. The next year, Smith's Gopher football career was depicted in the movie *Smith of Minnesota*.

After his graduation in 1942, Smith joined the navy. Following World War II, he played four seasons in the National Football League. Years later, *Minneapolis Tribune* columnist Dick Cullum wrote, "it would be difficult to find another occasion when one player so completely turned a game around from probable defeat to overwhelming victory as Smith did on that Iowa field."

After missing the previous two games because of injury, Bruce Smith sparked the Gophers' rally—including this kick by Pug Lund—against Iowa in the 1941 match-up.

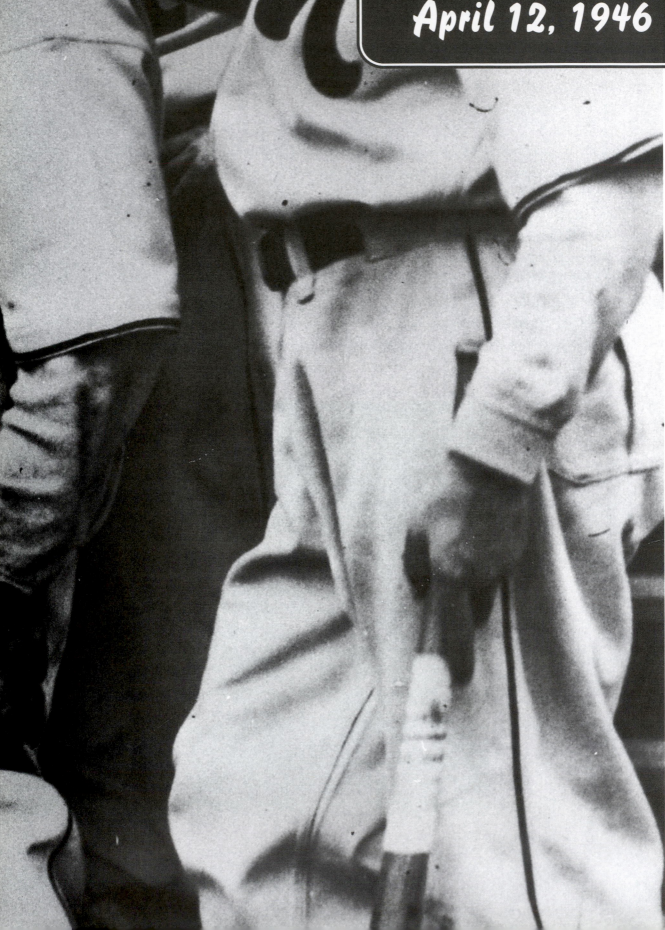

Kelley Era Comes to an End

Millers Owner Sells Team

It wasn't the first time a teenager had ignored a parent's advice. In 1895, nineteen-year-old Mike Kelley had been accepted to Harvard, Brown, Dartmouth, and Amherst, and his father urged him to attend one of the colleges and prepare for a profession like law or medicine. The younger Kelley, already noted for his skills as a baseball player, had a different idea. Ignoring his father's admonition to find a stable career, Kelley signed a contract to play professional baseball. For the next half-century—mostly in Minneapolis or St. Paul—baseball provided a steady income for Kelley.

A first baseman, Kelley embarked on his career by playing four seasons in minor leagues on the East Coast. In 1899, he joined the "major" National League when he played for Louisville, where he was a teammate of future Hall of Famer Honus Wagner. In 1900, Kelley joined Indianapolis of the American League, and the next year he managed Des Moines of the Western League. Kelley found a home in 1902 when he joined the St. Paul Saints of the American Association and, except for parts of two seasons, he was associated with the American Association for the next forty-four years.

In 1903, as a player-manager, Kelley led the Saints to the American Association pennant. (The Saints' second baseman was future New York Yankees manager and Hall of Famer Miller Huggins.) The Saints repeated as league champions the next year. Following the 1905 season, Kelley left the Saints after a falling-out with the owner and purchased the rival Minneapolis Millers for a reported twenty-five thousand dollars. But a dispute developed when the Saints' owner sold Kelley's contract to the St. Louis Browns of the American League. The matter was resolved in April 1906 when the National Association, the governing body of minor league baseball, overruled the Saints and Browns, clearing Kelley to manage the Millers.

After one controversial season [see pages 22–25], Kelley spent part of the 1907 season with Des Moines and started the 1908 season with Toronto of the International League. But in August 1908, Kelley rejoined the Saints. Except for the 1913 season, which he spent with

Mike Kelley, Judge Kenesaw Mountain Landis, and Joe Hauser gathered at the National Baseball Hall of Fame in Cooperstown, New York, in 1939.

Indianapolis, Kelley remained with the Saints until 1923. After a fifteen-year drought, the Saints won American Association titles in 1919, 1920, and 1922. The 1920 team, which compiled a 115–49 record, is considered one of the top ten minor-league teams of all time.

Following the 1923 season, Kelley returned to Minneapolis, partnering with two others to purchase the Millers. Kelley managed the next seven seasons before deciding to concentrate on front-office duties for the final fifteen years of his career. In thirty seasons as a minor-league manager, Kelley saw his teams win five pennants and compile a 2,390–2,102 record (.532 winning percentage). Only two other managers have won more games in the history of minor league baseball.

On April 12, just days before the start of the 1946 regular season, Kelley sold the Millers to Horace Stoneham, the owner of the New York Giants, thereby ending an era. One of the last independent minor-league team operators, Kelley retained the title of team president until the following January. After his retirement, Judge Kenesaw Mountain Landis, the com-

Mike Kelley owned the Minneapolis Millers from 1923 to 1946. Managed by Donie Bush, the 1935 Millers, shown here, won the American Association pennant.

missioner of major league baseball, praised Kelley as "one of the most truthful and honored men ever associated with baseball."

His father would have been proud.

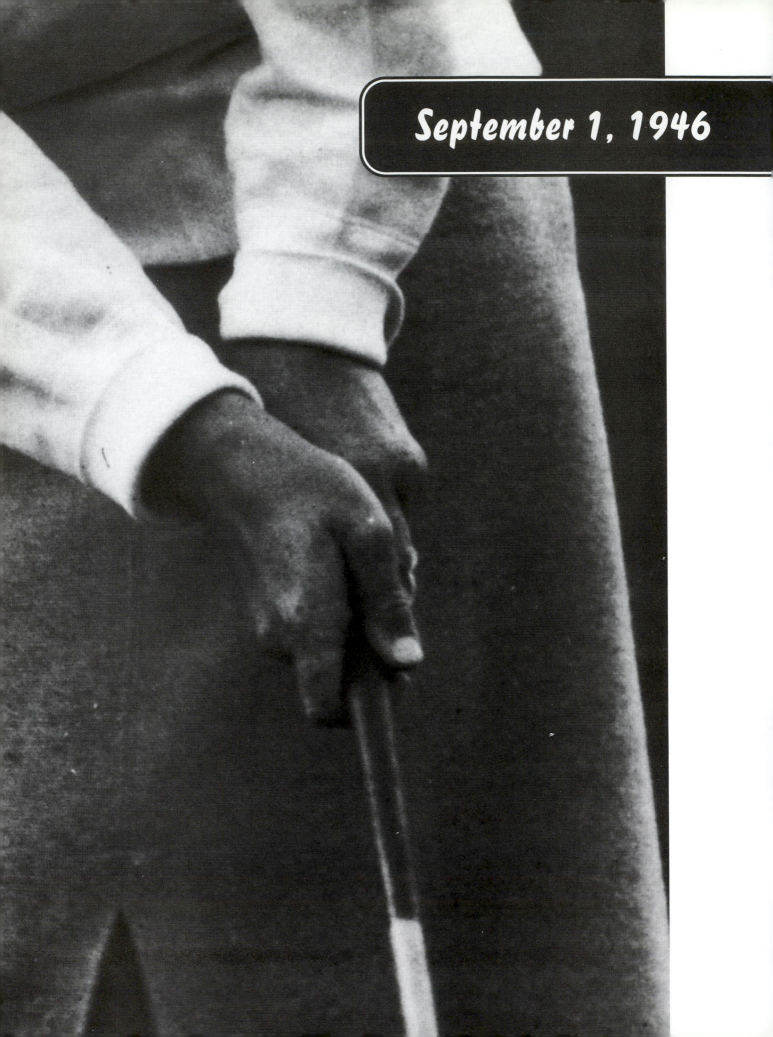

Luck Wins Open

Patty Berg Claims First Women's Golf Title

In the year following the end of World War II, Patty Berg was getting re-acquainted with her golf game. The Minneapolis native had turned professional in June 1940 after winning twenty-eight amateur championships in the preceding seven years. She won her first professional championship in 1941 and earned two other tournament titles that year before a knee injury, suffered in an automobile accident, caused her to miss eighteen months of golf.

The *Associated Press* female athlete of the year in 1938 and 1943, Berg enlisted in the Marine Corps in 1943 and was eventually commissioned a lieutenant. While in the service, Berg didn't find much time for golf, practicing no more than twice a week during a twenty-five-month span. But Berg still managed to win two tournaments in 1943, the Western Open and All-American Open, and one in 1945, the All-American. After being discharged from military service in September 1945, she resumed her professional career the next year by winning three tournaments in California. In late August 1946, Berg traveled to Spokane, Washington, to compete in the first U.S. Women's Open. The six-day tournament was offering the largest purse ever seen in women's professional golf—$19,700.

Berg, who started golfing at the age of thirteen, shot a 36-hole, three-under-par 145 to earn medalist honors in the open's qualifying round on August 27. Babe Didrikson Zaharias, a two-time gold medalist in track and field at the 1932 Olympics who had taken up golf in 1935, was second—eight strokes behind Berg.

After the qualifying round, the tournament switched to a 36-hole match-play format. In the first round of match play, Berg defeated Margaret Speer of Fort Leavenworth, Kansas, 7-and-6, while Zaharias lost her match. In the second round, Berg, who trailed by one after the front nine, rallied for a 5-and-3 victory over Marty Mozel of Portland, Oregon. Berg then defeated Hawaiian Jackie Pung 6-and-5, making her next stop the semifinals. Dot Kielty,

Before becoming a golf legend, Patty Berg played on a neighborhood football team called the Fiftieth Street Tigers. One of her Tiger teammates was future college football coaching legend Bud Wilkinson.

also from Minneapolis, reached the semifinals as well. Berg advanced to Sunday's finals with a 3-and-2 victory over amateur Betty Jean Rucker, who was playing on her home course, but an all-Minneapolis final didn't materialize as San Antonio's Betty Jameson edged Kielty, 1-up.

On September 1, after the first eighteen holes of the championship round, Berg and Jameson were tied. But Berg opened the final eighteen by winning five of the first six holes, relying on her strength by one-putting four times in that span. The match ended on the thirty-second hole of the day with Berg winning by a 5-and-4 margin.

Hal Wood of the *Associated Press* reported, "golf's payoff is in putting—and that's why Patty Berg, first women's national open golf champion today counted a fat bankroll of $5,600. In trouble a half-dozen times during the afternoon round Sunday from off-slant drives or weak approaches, Miss Berg either canned the putt when she got on the green or rolled the ball so close to the cup that it was a 'gimme.' Included in her quota were an 18-footer on the 16th, a 10-footer on the 17th, a seven-foot putt on 21, a 25-footer on 28, another for eight feet in 30 and a seven-foot effort on 32."

Berg celebrated the tournament victory by returning home to Minneapolis to see family and friends. "It takes 50 percent luck to win any big golf tournament," Berg told the *Minneapolis Tribune,* "but I had more than 50 percent this time. I want to hit a few with Les Bolstad [long-time golf coach at the University of Minnesota and her advisor for forty years] while I'm here. I never win a tournament that I don't thank him for it."

With the rust gone from her game, Berg went on to win forty-four titles between 1948 and 1962. Besides the numerous titles and records, she left a lasting imprint on women's professional golf. In 1950, Berg was one of the founding members of the Ladies Professional Golf Association, and she served as the group's first president.

Minneapolis native Patty Berg won twenty-eight golf tournaments as an amateur before turning professional in 1940.

November 19, 1947

Lakers Blossom into Winners

George Mikan Signs with Team

When it comes to basketball, George Mikan could be called a late bloomer. He was cut from his high school basketball team. One college coach wasn't interested in him because he was too awkward and wore glasses. He told Mikan he'd make a better scholar than a basketball player. Mikan was too tall and his eyesight too poor for him to enter the military. But after arriving at DePaul University, he blossomed into the nation's premier college basketball player, earning All-American honors three times. And in 1947, after being transplanted to Minneapolis, the six-foot-ten Mikan immediately transformed the Minneapolis Lakers, professional basketball's worst team the previous season, into one of the best in the country.

The Lakers spent the 1946–47 season as the Detroit Gems of the National Basketball League. Following a disastrous season, which saw the Gems win just one of their final twenty-eight games and compile a 4–40 record, the team's owner wanted to cut his losses. At the same time, a group of Minneapolis investors—represented by a young newspaper reporter named Sid Hartman—was looking for a basketball team to buy. The Minneapolis group paid fifteen thousand dollars for the Gems, and with their investment they acquired the Gems' poor record, guaranteeing a first selection in the league's draft.

Having done their homework, Hartman and the Minneapolis group focused on one player for that draft choice: Mikan, who was playing for Chicago's American Gears. After winning the NBL title in 1947, the Gears joined the new Professional Basketball League of America, which folded just two weeks into the 1947–48 season, making Mikan available. While several teams were interested in Mikan, Hartman knew that the Lakers retained the

Three-time All-American George Mikan helped the Minneapolis Lakers become a dynasty after he joined the team in 1947.

The Minneapolis Lakers, shown here in 1950, won six championships with George Mikan in the lineup.

NBL's draft rights. Six days after the PBLA folded, Mikan and his attorney arrived in Minneapolis to talk to Lakers officials. But after a day of negotiating failed to produce a contract, Mikan was ready to return to Chicago.

The Lakers officials knew that if Mikan left Minneapolis without a contract the two sides would likely never reach an agreement. Hartman put a plan into action, offering to drive Mikan to the airport, where he would catch the day's last flight. Hartman took his time on the drive, showing Mikan some of the sights of the city and arriving at the airport too late for the Chicago flight. The next day, the two sides signed a contract and, without the benefit of a practice, Mikan joined his new teammates in Sheboygan, Wisconsin, making his debut for the Lakers that very night.

Sheboygan pulled away in the second half for a 56–41 victory over the Lakers, who had won three of their first four games. Leading 23–19 at halftime, Sheboygan allowed the Lakers just eleven field goals, limiting Mikan to only three, but he made ten of eleven free throws to finish with a game-high 16 points.

The Lakers lost their first five games with Mikan, but after that inauspicious start they went on to win the NBL title, the first of six for the team. Mikan was later named the top basketball player of the first half of the twentieth century. Not a bad showing for an awkward kid with poor eyesight.

May 22, 1948
Campy Breaks a Barrier

Roy Campanella Debuts
with St. Paul Saints

Most minor league baseball teams would be elated with the addition of a top prospect to their roster. But in May 1948, the St. Paul Saints didn't cheer the news that the Brooklyn Dodgers were sending their top catching prospect—Roy Campanella—to St. Paul to gain experience.

The Saints were less than enthusiastic about the move for several reasons. After winning 16 of their previous 20 games, the Saints were in first place in the American Association, and they worried that roster changes would upset their team chemistry. Joe Hennessy mused in the *St. Paul Pioneer Press*, "[Brooklyn general manager Branch] Rickey does not intend to have Campanella—regarded as the top catching prospect in the minors—sit on the bench . . . [but] does Rickey want to break up a first-place team?"

Further, the Saints were satisfied with their catching duo. According to *St. Paul Dispatch* columnist George Edmond, "the Saints didn't need catching with both Farrell Anderson and Stew Hoffarth around." He went on to note, "But neither did the other top Brooklyn farm teams. As a top major-league prospect, Campanella has to be kept working." Also in the *Dispatch*, Mark Tierney wrote, "[manager Walt] Alston will find it hard to bench one of his regulars." Particularly Anderson, who was hitting .336.

So Campanella joined the Saints with something to prove. In the process, he made history. Edmond wrote about the significance of Campanella's arrival:

> Just as Jackie Robinson was welcomed by fans when he joined the Brooklyn club, so will virtually all Saint fans welcome the precedent-breaking addition of Campanella. The new Saint catcher will be the first African-American ever to play in the [46 years] of the American Association, but he has played in Montreal. He was

Future Hall of Famer Roy Campanella became the first African American to play in the American Association when he joined the St. Paul Saints in 1948.

well-received there and around the rest of the International League. With African Americans now playing in both major leagues and all three Triple-A leagues, another step in the break-down of race prejudice, which got its greatest momentum as a result of the war, has been taken.

On May 22, Campanella joined the Saints in Columbus, Ohio, making his debut in a game won by the Redbirds 13–5, behind future major-leaguer Harvey Haddix's eight-hitter. In its account of the game, the *Associated Press* described Campanella's historic debut: "He fanned twice and went hitless in four trips, besides having a throwing error trying to pick a Redbird off second base."

After this lackluster start, things quickly improved for Campanella. The next day, he caught the second game of a double-header—going 1-for-3 in the Saints' 2–1 victory. Over the next month, Campanella displayed the potential the Dodgers had envisioned. On June 30, after going 4-for-8 in the Saints' double-header split in Toledo, he was recalled by the Dodgers. Campanella batted .325 with 13 home runs and 39 RBIs in 35 games for the Saints. In Brooklyn, the future Hall of Famer quickly assumed the starting catcher's role—one he held for the next ten seasons.

Roy Campanella hit 13 home runs in 35 games for the Saints, including this one against the Minneapolis Millers at Nicollet Park. Manager Walt Alston congratulates Campanella as he rounds third.

April 12, 1954

The End of a Dynasty

Minneapolis Lakers Take Final Title

"Dynasty" and "superstar" are two of the most overused words in sports. But before the Boston Celtics of the 1960s and long before players like Wilt Chamberlain, Magic Johnson, or Michael Jordan, the National Basketball Association had its first dynasty and superstar—the Minneapolis Lakers and their six-foot-ten center, George Mikan.

The Lakers were the biggest attraction in the early days of the NBA. An exhibition game between the Lakers and the Harlem Globetrotters at Chicago Stadium drew a record crowd of 20,004. Mikan's dominance was so complete that the league altered the rules, widening the lanes and adopting a shot clock. He was so well known that when the Lakers traveled to New York to play the Knicks, the marquee outside Madison Square Garden read, "Geo. Mikan vs. Knicks."

The Lakers and Mikan had earned their reputations. In 1947–48, their first year of existence, they won the National Basketball League title. The next season they won the Basketball Association of America title, and when the BAA renamed itself the National Basketball Association the next year, they earned their third consecutive title. In 1951, the Lakers' run was stopped by the Rochester Royals in the West Division finals, the loss ending the Lakers' streak of victories in twelve consecutive play-off series. But the Lakers regrouped and won titles in 1952 and 1953.

At the start of the 1953–54 season, some NBA observers wondered if the Lakers would maintain their dynasty. Compiling a league-best 46–26 record during the regular season, the Lakers showed that their reign was not over. For the 1954 play-offs, the league introduced a new format, with the top three teams in each division playing a round robin to determine each division's two finalists. The Lakers defeated Rochester and Fort Wayne to advance to the West Division finals against Rochester. The Lakers overpowered Rochester 2–1 in a best-of-three series to advance to the NBA finals against the East Division champion Syracuse Nationals.

The finals—a best-of-seven series—opened in Minneapolis on March 31 with the Lakers winning 79–68. But the Nationals, who had finished second in the East during the regular season, proved to be a formidable foe, evening the series with a victory in game two, and then, following Lakers' victories in games three and five, tying the series each time. Winning game six in Minneapolis 65–63, the Nationals forced a seventh game.

On April 12, the Lakers finally overcame the Nationals. Before a Minneapolis Auditorium crowd of 7,274, the Lakers never trailed after taking an 8–7 lead. Ahead by six points at halftime and by as many as 16 in the third quarter, the Lakers finally settled for an 87–80 victory. Jim Pollard scored 21 points and Slater Martin added 14 to lead the Lakers. The Nats held Mikan to just two field goals and 11 points, but Mikan grabbed 15 rebounds and rookie Clyde Lovelette contributed 14 points and 13 rebounds for the Lakers. Mikan and Lovelette helped the Lakers to a 56–38 rebound advantage.

The next day, more than four hundred people turned out to honor the Lakers at a luncheon at the Nicollet Hotel. The *Minneapolis Tribune* reported NBA president Maurice Podoloff's remarks to the crowd: "One can only deal with superlatives in discussing this team. I will say that it is the greatest team in the history of basketball and deserves a place

---

The Minneapolis Lakers won their third consecutive NBA championship in 1954. Front row, from left: Max Winter, Jim Pollard, George Mikan (holding trophy), coach John Kundla, Bob Harrison, Don Carlson, Slater Martin, and Buddy Hassett (kneeling). Back row: Sid Hartman, Herman Schaefer, Vern Mikkelsen (just visible behind Schaefer), Bud Grant, Arnie Ferrin, and Tony Jaros.

The Lakers' championship run – six in seven seasons – came to an end in 1954. The 1955–56 Lakers, shown here, finished with a 33–39 record.

not earned by any team in any type of athletics. The Lakers have been the greatest contributing factor to the success of the NBA. Names of the players are a household word all over the nation. The record of the Minneapolis Lakers—winning six world titles in seven years—will remain unchallenged for years to come. I am looking forward with pleasure to coming back here for many years to come."

While Podoloff was right about the Lakers' impact on the league, he was wrong about return trips to Minneapolis. The sixth title was the last for the Lakers. Mikan retired shortly before the start of the next season at the age of twenty-nine. He made a brief comeback, playing thirty-seven games in the 1955–56 season, but his exit signaled the end of the league's first dynasty.

Doug Gillen crosses home plate and is congratulated by other members of the 1956 Gopher baseball team, the first to earn a conference championship in twenty-one years.

Gophers Triumphant in College World Series

Dick Siebert entered his ninth year as the University of Minnesota baseball coach with a lot of uncertainty. In fall 1955, Siebert didn't know if five players he was counting on for big contributions would be with the team when the spring season opened. Two players had eligibility issues, two were debating whether to pass up baseball for spring football practice, and one had an arm injury. With these three position players and two pitchers in the lineup, the Gophers expected to continue the success they had enjoyed the previous season, when they won a school-record twenty-three games and finished second in the Big Ten, their best conference finish in twelve years. Without that group, the Gophers would be short-handed.

Eventually the five—second baseman Gene Martin, outfielders Bill Horning and Dave Lindblom, and pitchers Dean Maas and Rod Oistad—resolved their issues and joined the team. Each would make his own contribution to what became the best baseball season in school history.

As they had in Siebert's first eight years as coach, the Gophers opened their season in late March with a trip to Texas, winning three of eight games on the trip. After returning home, they continued their preparation for the conference season with eight consecutive nonconference victories. But the Gophers began and ended their 1956 conference schedule with losses. In between those two defeats—on April 27 to Wisconsin and on May 25 to Ohio State—they won eleven straight conference games to compile an 11–2 Big Ten mark and earn their first conference championship in twenty-one years. During May, the Gophers also won two nonconference games, giving them a 21–2 record since returning home from their spring trip.

The conference title also earned the Gophers the first baseball postseason berth in school history. But the postseason started the way the regular season had ended—with a

Jerry Thomas, Rod Oistad, and Ron Craven were the mainstays of the Gophers' pitching staff in 1956.

loss. On May 29, Notre Dame defeated the Gophers 4–3 in the first game of their best-of-three District IV play-off series in Minneapolis. The Gophers recovered to defeat the Irish twice the next day—15–5 and 10–1—to advance to the region finals against Ohio University. The Gophers traveled to Athens, Ohio, where they defeated the Bobcats 5–0 and 7–6 to earn their first trip to the College World Series, in Omaha, Nebraska.

Having won 25 of their last 28 games, the Gophers took a 28–8 record into the eight-team, double-elimination tournament, and they stayed hot in Omaha. Starting on June 9, the Gophers defeated Wyoming 4–0, Arizona 3–1, Mississippi 13–5, and Bradley 8–3 to reach the championship round.

After losing to the Gophers, Arizona fought its way back through the losers' bracket to earn another shot at Minnesota. And on June 13, Arizona defeated the Gophers 10–4, handing them their first loss in the double-elimination tournament and forcing a second game for the championship. The next day, before a crowd of 3,890, Jerry Thomas allowed just five hits, pitching the Gophers to a 12–1 victory over the Wildcats. The Gophers supported Thomas, who was named most outstanding player of the tournament, with fourteen hits. Leading 4–0 after four innings, they broke the game open with a six-run fifth inning. Horning, one of those question marks for Siebert at the start of the school year, hit two home runs and drove in five. Thomas, who had allowed just three hits in the Gophers' 3–1 victory over Arizona in the second round, struck out four and retired the Wildcats in order in six of nine innings.

Siebert told the *Minneapolis Tribune*'s Sid Hartman, "I said before the season that you needed luck to go all the way and we had our share. But this team was a great bunch of competitors. They had outstanding leadership from Horning. I never saw a closer knit group. And they played harder when it counted most."

The Gophers won 30 of their final 34 games. Shortstop Jerry Kindall, who signed a pro contract shortly after the tournament, led the Gophers with eighteen home runs. In conference games, Kindall batted .440 with six home runs. The season that began with many question marks ushered in a highly successful era during which the Gophers won three national titles in eight years.

October 6, 1959
A Revolutionary Junior World Series

Millers Travel to Havana

Minor league baseball's Junior World Series, between the champions of the International League and the American Association, had been played since 1904. But with players building fires in the dugout for warmth in one city and armed soldiers patrolling the field in the other, the 1959 Junior World Series between the Minneapolis Millers and the Havana Sugar Kings proved to be one of the most memorable.

The Millers, a Boston Red Sox farm team managed by Gene Mauch, had finished second in the American Association's East Division despite winning ninety-five games. In the American Association play-offs, the Millers defeated West Division champion Omaha four games to two and then defeated Fort Worth four games to three to earn their second consecutive berth in the Junior World Series.

The Sugar Kings, a Cincinnati Reds farm team managed by Preston Gomez, had finished third in the International League regular season. But in the first round of the I.L. play-offs, the Sugar Kings swept second-place Columbus (managed by Cal Ermer), and then defeated Richmond, which had stunned regular-season champion Buffalo in the other first-round series, four games to two.

The seven-game series between the Millers and the Sugar Kings was scheduled to begin on Sunday, September 27, with the first three games of the series—on Sunday afternoon and Monday and Tuesday nights—played in Metropolitan Stadium in Bloomington. Then the series would move to Havana for the final four games.

Behind Ted Wieand's six-hitter, the Sugar Kings won the series opener 5–2 before 2,486 fans at the Met. The contest became a little more interesting the following night. On a cool and windy evening, a crowd of only 1,065 saw the Millers slug four home runs, including

The Minneapolis Millers reached the Junior World Series four times. The 1959 team, shown here, made the final trip – all the way to Havana.

Eddie Sadowski's leadoff in the bottom of the ninth, to defeat the Sugar Kings 6–5. With the series even, the third game, scheduled for 8:15 P.M. Tuesday, was postponed because of the temperature—it was a brisk forty-seven degrees—and officials elected to move the rest of the series to Havana. The Sugar Kings, unaccustomed to the climate, had built fires in their dugout for warmth during the first two games.

American Association president Ed Doherty explained the decision to the *Minneapolis Tribune:* "The commission [comprised of Doherty, president George Trautman of the minor leagues, and International League president Frank Shaughnessy] had no choice but to cancel Tuesday night's game in Minneapolis because of cold weather. In fairness to the players, who share in the receipts from the first four games, we decided to move the rest of the series to Havana where the weather is favorable and the interest is great."

In Cuba, the series was of interest to the entire island, especially to a former baseball player named Fidel Castro, Cuba's political leader. When the series resumed two days later, an enthusiastic crowd of 24,988, including Castro, turned out for the game. The Sugar Kings outlasted the Millers 3–2 in ten innings to take a 2–1 lead in the series. According to the *Minneapolis Tribune,* on Friday, October 2, Castro cancelled a cabinet meeting so he and

other high government officials could attend the fourth game. The Sugar Kings won again in extra innings, 3–1 in eleven, to move within one victory of taking the series.

But with soldiers stationed in the dugouts and lining the field to demonstrate Castro's power, the Millers regrouped and won the next two games, 4–2 and 5–3, to tie the series and force a deciding seventh game. Adding to the drama, the final game was rained out on Monday, October 5. "I'd just as soon have played it and got this thing over with," Mauch told the *Tribune*. The next day, in front of another overflow crowd of twenty thousand, the Sugar Kings rallied for a 3–2 victory. Trailing 2–0 after seven innings, the Kings scored twice in the eighth to tie the game and then won in the ninth. Following the final out, the elated fans swarmed the field around Castro's box, chanting, "Fidel, Fidel."

The series went down in the record books as the attendance champion of the Junior

Members of the Havana Sugar Kings try to stay warm in their Metropolitan Stadium dugout during the second game of the 1959 Junior World Series. The next night's game was postponed because of cold weather, and the rest of the series was moved to Havana.

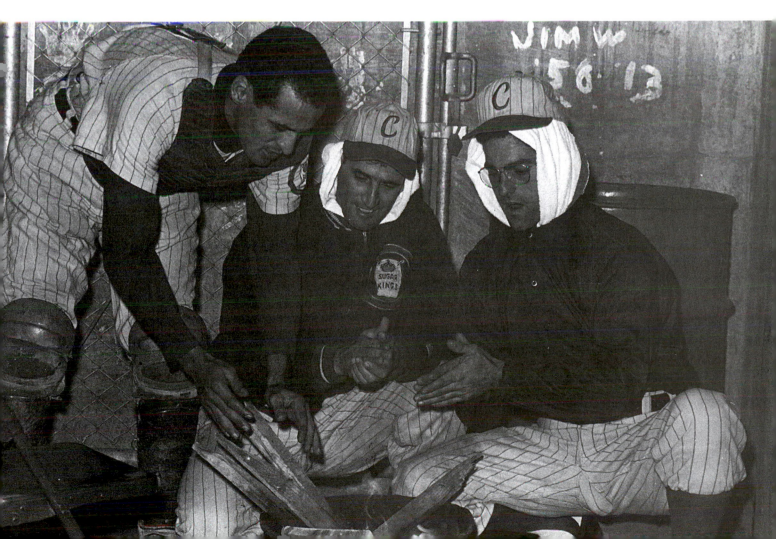

World Series: 103,808 people watched the seven-game series—more than 100,000 in the five games in Havana.

Years later, Millers pitcher Ted Bowsfield recalled the scene for author Stew Thornley: "Nobody minded losing the game in that country and under those conditions. We were just happy to get out of town with our hides. During every game we could hear shots being fired and we never knew what was going on." The Millers' Lefty Locklin told Thornley, "When Castro made his entrance [before the seventh game, he] passed the Minneapolis players in the bullpen, put his hand on his revolver and said, 'tonight, we win.'"

After a cold start, the series certainly provided a lot of "warm" memories. The following season was the final one for both teams: the Sugar Kings moved to Jersey City and the Millers gave way to major league baseball.

NFL Votes to Expand, Grants Franchise to Minnesota

After obtaining a professional basketball franchise—the Minneapolis Lakers—in 1947, Twin Cities civic leaders set out the next year to secure a professional football or major league baseball team for the area. Over the next dozen years, Minnesotans played a waiting game as the quest for a franchise involved various leagues. In the 1950s, the New York Giants of the National League, the Philadelphia Athletics, St. Louis Browns, and Washington Senators of the American League, and the Chicago Cardinals of the National Football League all entertained the idea of moving to the Twin Cities. After several disappointments, the outlook brightened for Minneapolis and St. Paul in 1959.

That July, a group of New York businessmen, frustrated with major league baseball's reluctance to expand, announced it would form a third major baseball league. The eight-team league, dubbed the Continental League and scheduled to begin play in 1961, awarded a franchise to the Twin Cities [see pages 103–4]. Then in November, a group equally frustrated by the National Football League's unwillingness to add to its twelve franchises announced it would form a second professional football league. The American Football League held its first full league meeting in Minneapolis on November 22. During the meeting, business-man Max Winter, former owner of the Minneapolis Lakers, announced he was planning to field a team in the league, which would begin play in 1960.

On the same day, a crowd of 26,625 gathered at Metropolitan Stadium to watch the New York Giants defeat the Chicago Cardinals 30–20, the Cardinal's second regular-season game in the Twin Cities that year. Both the AFL meeting and the Giants-Cardinals game made an impression on the NFL. In January 1960, NFL owners convened in Miami. Their first order of business: elect a new commissioner, thirty-three-year-old Pete Rozelle. The second: tackle the expansion question.

Four months earlier—at the funeral for Bert Bell, for fourteen years the league's commissioner—the league's owners authorized George Halas, chairman of the expansion committee, to consider the issue. The NFL hadn't expanded since 1950, when it absorbed three teams from the All-America Football Conference. After hours of debate in Miami, the owners took the first step toward expanding, passing an amendment to the league's bylaws reducing from twelve (unanimous) to ten the number of votes required to admit new franchises. The next day, the owners debated adding teams. Undoubtedly influenced by the threat of an AFL team moving into the Upper Midwest, Halas, the owner of the Chicago Bears, successfully urged the other eleven owners to expand.

Coach Norm Van Brocklin (kneeling) and four prospects huddle during the Vikings' first training camp in 1961. Rookie quarterback Fran Tarkenton is second from the left.

According to the *Minneapolis Tribune*'s Sid Hartman, in the afternoon of January 28, Rozelle gathered reporters in a hotel lobby and said, "Gentlemen, I have an announcement to make. Dallas has been voted into the NFL for 1960. And the Twin Cities of Minneapolis–St. Paul will be activated in 1961."

Winter was surprised, telling the *Minneapolis Star,* "We appeared to be rebuffed at every turn while the owners were trying to pick a new commissioner. Then when they got into the franchise matter, it appeared that we would be shut out. In fact, at noon I thought we were licked. Apparently there was a last-minute move to pass up the Twin Cities. But at 2 P.M. came the good news. Naturally, I was overwhelmed because we have fought so long to reach this goal."

As Hartman reported in the *Tribune,* New York Giants owner Tim Mara indicated that the sellout between the Giants and Cardinals convinced the other NFL owners to look closely at the Twin Cities area.

In addition to the expansion fee of six hundred thousand dollars, the franchise had to meet two conditions before beginning play in 1961: sell twenty-five thousand season tickets and expand Metropolitan Stadium to forty thousand seats. Elated at their success, the Minnesota ownership group of Winter, Bernie Ridder, H. P. Skoglund, Ole Haugsrud, and Bill Boyer didn't mind having a year to prepare.

February 27–28, 1960
Miracle on Ice, Part I

U.S. Wins Hockey Gold

Two periods into the 1960 Olympic gold medal hockey game, the U.S. team, which had been the surprise of the games, was losing and appeared tired. Considering they were playing at 8 A.M. after battling through six games—including the previous night against Russia—in the 6,200-foot altitude of Squaw Valley, California, their exhaustion was understandable.

The Americans, including eight Minnesotans, were trailing Czechoslovakia, a team they had beaten by two goals in the first round, 4–3. The Czechs had needed just eight seconds to score their first goal, and they added two more in that first period. But the Americans recovered in the third after some advice from an unlikely source. In between periods, Nikolai Sologubov, the captain of the Russian team upset by the Americans in the semifinals the night before, visited the U.S. locker room and urged coach Jack Riley to have his players use oxygen. Sologubov even helped administer oxygen to members of the team.

The rejuvenated Americans scored six goals in the final period—three made by Warroad's Roger Christian—to stun Czechoslovakia 9–4 and earn the gold medal in hockey for the first time. "Credit Solly [Sologubov] for helping us win the championship. It was his idea," Riley told the *Associated Press*. "Most of our guys didn't sleep last night from excitement and tension. And when we had an early 8 A.M. game we were kind of tired. The oxygen sure came in handy. We never used it before." Christian added, "Solly helped us all right. But it was the gold medal that spurred us on. Remember that."

Riley credited Christian, who scored the game-tying goal five minutes into the third period, with the game's turning point. Two minutes later, Bob Cleary scored to put the Americans ahead. Then Team U.S.A. broke the game open with three goals—by Bob Cleary, Christian, and Billy Cleary—in a 67-second span. Christian completed the scoring with two minutes remaining.

Brothers Billy, Gordy, and Roger Christian of Warroad were members of the 1960 U.S. Olympic hockey team.

The gold medal surprised the Americans, who had won the silver at the 1956 games in Italy but hadn't been expected to accomplish much at the 1960 games. After opening-round victories over Australia (12–1) and Czechoslovakia (7–5), the United States defeated favored Sweden 6–3 with three goals from Roger Christian and three assists from his brother Billy. The Americans then routed Germany 9–1 before outlasting Canada, one of the favorites, 2–1 in the quarterfinals. In the semifinals, in front of nine thousand fans, the Americans avenged a 4–0 loss to the Russians in the 1956 gold medal game with a 3–2 victory. With Team U.S.A. trailing 2–1 in the second period, Billy Christian tied the game and then broke

the tie with five minutes remaining in the third period. Goalie Jack McCartan, who played baseball and hockey at the University of Minnesota, made thirty-one saves and was named the most outstanding player of the tournament.

Minneapolis Tribune columnist Dick Cullum commented on the semifinal game: "Isn't it safe to say that the United States–Russia hockey game was television's finest moment in sports? If you dispute this, then name another occasion when a single event meant so much to so many and was followed with such intensity of nationwide interest." Cullum's argument was safe for twenty years [see pages 172–74].

The U.S. Olympic hockey team celebrates after defeating Czechoslovakia 9–4 to capture the gold medal in 1960.

March 27, 1960

Tiny Edgerton Amazes State

Flying Dutchmen Claim Basketball Title

By 1960, the Minnesota boys' state basketball tournament had become one of the nation's top sporting events, its three-day competition drawing nearly eighty-five thousand fans. After a tournament attendance mark was set in 1959, the record was broken the next year, when the biggest attraction was the smallest school. Unheralded Edgerton, from a community of less than one thousand in southwestern Minnesota, brought an unblemished 24–0 record to the 1960 competition. Despite their unbeaten record, the Dutchmen weren't mentioned as one of the pre-tourney favorites, with most observers focusing on Austin and Richfield.

Edgerton, Austin, Richfield, and Granite Falls were the winners on the opening day of the tournament. In the semifinals, Austin defeated Granite Falls while Edgerton surprised Richfield 63–60, setting the stage for the forty-eighth boys' state basketball championship game. On Saturday, March 27, a crowd of 19,018—a record attendance for a high school basketball game in Minnesota—filled Williams Arena on the University of Minnesota campus to watch Austin, one of the biggest high schools in the state, take on Edgerton.

Making its thirteenth state tournament appearance in twenty seasons under coach Ove Berven, Austin had the edge in experience. But the Flying Dutchmen and their twenty-three-year-old rookie coach Richie Olson had the support of the crowd. When the Packers, who had won the tournament two years earlier, took the floor before the championship game, they were greeted by a chorus of boos, which continued throughout the game after every Austin point or foul.

Edgerton coach Richie Olson, Edgerton mayor John DeVoer, and leading scorer Dean Veenhof greet the hometown crowd after the 1960 state basketball tournament.

The Flying Dutchmen surround coach Richie Olson after defeating Austin 72–61 at Williams Arena before 19,018 – the largest crowd to watch a high school basketball game in Minnesota.

In control from the outset, the Flying Dutchmen led by six points after the first quarter, opened a 12-point lead at halftime, and extended it to 17 in the second half before settling for a 72–61 victory. The Dutchmen made 55 percent of their field goal attempts (26 of 47) to become the smallest school to win the state championship since Gaylord in 1926. They were led by six-foot-five junior Dean Veenhof, who scored a game-high 26 points. Three other Edgerton players scored in double figures—LeRoy Graphenteen (15 points), Dean Verdoes (12), and Darrell Kreun (11).

Columnist Charles Johnson commented on the winners the next day in the *Minneapolis Sunday Tribune:* "Edgerton's state championship basketball team must go down in history as one of the most amazing organizations that ever set the pace in the prep parade. This was a team victory that will live long in the memory of those fortunate enthusiasts who managed to get at least one look at Edgerton through three sessions. No more popular victory ever was registered in this classic. No one team ever merited all the honors more than the Dutchmen from southwestern Minnesota."

But Johnson also chastised the raucous crowd: "Even though Edgerton was everyone's favorite, there is no place in sports for the crowd's treatment of the game fighters from Austin. [The Packers] must wonder how any sports crowd could act the way this one did." He added his assessment of the Packers, who "rated with some of the best runners-up this event ever has had."

The Austin coach downplayed the crowd's effect. "We've been booed before and I'd be the last to say it would affect the play of our team," Berven said. "[Edgerton] is a team you have to see to believe."

Indeed: more than four decades later, Minnesota high school basketball fans are still talking about Edgerton.

Departing for Warmer Climes

Lakers Desert Minneapolis for Los Angeles

Beginning in 1947, the Minneapolis Lakers' stay in Minnesota was marked by tremendous glory and constant uncertainty. Led by George Mikan, the team won six championships in a seven-season span. But off the court, the Lakers were plagued by questions over facilities and finances.

Unable to call one arena "home," the Lakers shuttled between three inadequate facilities—the Minneapolis Auditorium, the Minneapolis Armory, and the St. Paul Auditorium. Additionally, in the late 1950s, while their financial problems grew, the Lakers' schedule frequently took a back seat to conventions and expositions at the Minneapolis Auditorium. Bob Short, who purchased the team in 1957, sought to remedy the situation. In spring 1960—three months after a twelve-year quest to secure a professional football franchise had ended fruitfully for the Twin Cities—Short admitted that he had been unable to devise a local solution to the Lakers' arena problems.

Short found his answer on the West Coast, announcing on April 26 that he had reached a tentative agreement to move his famous franchise to Los Angeles for the following season. Short told Dick Cullum of the *Minneapolis Tribune,* "We are not planning to move just to move. We would not consider any other city but Los Angeles. Prospects there are so bright that ordinary business judgment, considering our financial state, compels us to favor that city."

But the proposed move wasn't immediately endorsed. One day after the announcement, the league's owners convened in New York City to consider Short's plight. Wary of increased travel costs to shuttle their teams to the West Coast, the owners voted 7–1 against Short's request to relocate. Moments after the vote, the owners learned that Abe Saperstein had

The Minneapolis Lakers, shown here in 1955, played their home games at three different venues in the Twin Cities – the Minneapolis Auditorium, the Minneapolis Armory, and the St. Paul Auditorium – before moving to Los Angeles in 1960.

announced the formation of the American Basketball League, which would begin play in fall 1960 with teams in Cleveland, Kansas City, Los Angeles, San Francisco, and Washington. The owners, concerned about losing the Los Angeles market to a rival league, quickly reconvened and re-voted, this time unanimously approving the Lakers' move.

"I wanted to stay in Minneapolis, but could find no way of making it a financially sound investment," Short told Tom Briere of the *Minneapolis Tribune*. "The hopes of making it a Minneapolis–St. Paul ven-

The Lakers and the Detroit Pistons are shown in action during a 1958 contest. The Pistons finished second and the Lakers fourth in the West Division.

ture with games at Williams Arena failed when I could make no headway in guaranteeing use of the university building. Naturally, I have mixed emotions. I'm disappointed I couldn't make a go of it in Minneapolis, but other smart operators before me found it was too difficult and bowed out earlier. I'm delighted that Los Angeles was our solution."

The Lakers' new home would be the Los Angeles Sports Arena, where they had already played during a two-game West Coast series with the Philadelphia Warriors. On January 31, Wilt Chamberlain scored 41 points and had 32 rebounds, leading the Warriors to a 114–104 victory over the Lakers before 8,057 spectators in San Francisco. The next night the teams played in Los Angeles, with the Warriors defeating the Lakers 103–96 before 10,202 at the arena. With what the Lakers netted from the two games—and by trading Larry Foust to St. Louis for three players and ten thousand dollars—the financially challenged team was able to meet its immediate payroll obligations.

Finishing the regular season with a 25–50 record, the Lakers beat the Detroit Pistons twice to sweep their first-round, best-of-three play-off series and advance to the West Division finals, where they met the St. Louis Hawks. After a 117–110 overtime victory in St. Louis, the Lakers had a 3–2 lead in the best-of-seven series and were just one victory away from the NBA finals. But on March 24, before a record crowd of 9,544 at the Minneapolis Armory, St. Louis evened the series with a 117–96 victory, despite Elgin Baylor's heroic 38 points for the Lakers. Two nights later, St. Louis defeated the Lakers 97–86 to win the series.

A month after that, Short made his move. Cullum outlined the reasons in the *Minneapolis Tribune:* "We must face the fact that the Lakers did not have a fair chance here. They were denied suitable facilities. It has been nobody's fault, only a case of the town lacking suitable facilities. On a comparison of facilities alone, the move is justified."

The Lakers, the NBA's original dynasty, went on to create another dynasty after the move to L.A.

October 26, 1960
The Senators Are Coming

Twin Cities Finally Acquire Major League Team

Twin Cities moving companies must have kept pretty busy in 1960. In late January, a professional football franchise arrived. Three months later, the Minneapolis Lakers departed for the West Coast. Late in the year came another arrival—the Washington Senators.

After several years of speculation, Washington Senators owner Calvin Griffith finally announced on October 26 that he would relocate his American League franchise to the Twin Cities for the 1961 season. Twin Cities civic leaders had begun negotiations to lure the Senators from the nation's capital in 1957. The following July, Griffith reportedly was ready to ask American League owners for permission to relocate his team to Minnesota. But two days later, at a Congressional hearing about antitrust legislation, Griffith testified that he would never move the team. Two weeks after that hearing, Griffith and the Senators arrived in the Twin Cities—for an exhibition. The Senators defeated the Philadelphia Phillies 8–6 before 15,990 at Metropolitan Stadium.

In September 1958, Griffith again appeared ready to request permission to move, but he apparently changed his mind, announcing the team would remain in Washington for the 1959 season. Then, during the 1959 World Series, the *Sporting News* reported that the transfer of the Senators to the Twin Cities for the 1960 season was a certainty. Griffith dismissed the report as hearsay to Charles Johnson, the sports editor of both the *Minneapolis Tribune* and the *Minneapolis Star*. Johnson, in an article published October 3, 1959, quoted Griffith: "Our club has been talking with Minneapolis and St. Paul people on and off for the past two years. I understand a new offer is to be made to our organization. I haven't received it yet, but it would have to go through the regular channels. . . . We are always willing to listen to

Governor Orville Freeman (center) was among those who greeted Calvin Griffith in 1960 after Griffith announced he was relocating his baseball team to Minnesota.

any invitations to move where we can improve our position. Indirectly, I've had requests to talk with people in Louisville and Atlanta just as I have conversed with civic, business and sports leaders in the Twin Cities."

But all this talk didn't lead to a deal, and the Senators remained in Washington for the 1960 season. Speculation about expansion and/or franchise relocation heated up during the off-season. In mid-October, the National League owners voted to expand to ten teams by granting franchises to New York and Houston. American League owners convened in New York a week later for an "expansion and re-alignment session." The meeting produced dramatic changes, with the Senators moving to Minnesota, an expansion franchise awarded to Washington, D.C., to replace the Senators, and an expansion team for Los Angeles.

"I am relieved," Griffith told Johnson. "I have been sold on Minneapolis and St. Paul and the Upper Midwest for major league baseball from the first time I visited there almost three years ago. I felt this was the finest area in the country for a major-league team. You know for three years I have wanted to move up there. However, I want to make it clear, that today was the first time I officially asked the league to give me permission to move. On two other occasions, when I was set for such action, I was told by fellow club owners they wouldn't go along with me. As a result, I didn't make the proposal. But I never got Minneapolis and St. Paul out of my mind."

Minnesota governor Orville Freeman and Minnesota senator Hubert Humphrey both lauded the move in the *Minneapolis Tribune*. "Major-league baseball will be a real stimulus to a bigger and better Minnesota," said Freeman. Humphrey called the announcement, "A great day for the Twin Cities and a great day for Minnesota," adding, "A long struggle to bring major league baseball here has culminated in success."

The Twins quickly made themselves at home, earning three postseason appearances and leading the American League in attendance in their first ten seasons in Minnesota.

January 2, 1961
Vindication for the Gophers

Warmath Leads Team to Rose Bowl

At the end of the 1959 season, many University of Minnesota football fans were disillusioned with the Gophers. The program, which just a generation earlier had captured five national championships in an eight-season span, had won just three games in the 1958 and 1959 seasons combined. After the Gophers concluded a 2–7 season with an 11–7 loss to Wisconsin, some fans demonstrated their displeasure. Murray Warmath, who had coached the Gophers for six seasons, was hung in effigy outside a campus dormitory, and there were published reports of garbage being thrown on the lawn of his home.

Gopher fans had little reason to believe things would improve in 1960, and those doubts were reinforced when the team prepared for their 1960 regular-season opener against Nebraska by losing an exhibition game to a Gopher alumni team, 19–7. But the 1960 Gopher football team soon erased the memories of the previous two seasons by pulling off the biggest turnaround in the history of the program.

The Gophers rebounded from the exhibition loss by winning their first seven regular-season games. Unranked in preseason polls, the team slowly moved up to number three in the *Associated Press* Top 25—and the Gophers weren't done climbing. Following a convincing 27–10 victory over number-one-ranked and previously unbeaten Iowa in Iowa City, Minnesota took over the top spot in the *Associated Press* poll for the first time since November 1941. After reaching number one, the Gophers stumbled in their next-to-last regular-season game. Purdue, which brought a 2–4–1 record and a three-game losing streak to Minnesota, stunned the Gophers 23–14 before 61,348 at Memorial Stadium.

The loss dropped the Gophers to number four in the poll. They regrouped and closed out the regular season with a 26–7 victory over Wisconsin, a feat so impressive that they regained first place in the final regular-season poll—Minnesota's sixth national championship—and, more significantly, earned a bowl game invitation for the first time in school history.

On Monday, January 2, the top-ranked Gophers and number six Washington played before 97,314 in the Rose Bowl in Pasadena, California. The Huskies, who had beaten Wisconsin 44–8 in the 1960 Rose Bowl, scored two touchdowns in the second quarter to take a 17–0 lead at halftime. As they had all season, the Gophers showed their resiliency by scoring on the opening drive of the second half, narrowing the Huskies' lead to ten points. The

After winning just two games in 1959, the Gopher football team went 8–1 in 1960 to reach the Rose Bowl for the first time.

HAGBERG—M

BALL

FAR

Gopher fullback Roger Hagberg scores a touchdown against Purdue on November 14, 1960.

Gophers reached the Huskies' 6-yard line midway through the fourth quarter, but an interception ended the drive as the Huskies held on for a 17–7 victory. "We usually don't score a lot of points," Warmath told the *Minneapolis Tribune*. "Our strength has been our ability to stop the other team. But we couldn't stop Washington in the first half. As a result, we didn't get the ball."

The loss didn't diminish a remarkable turnaround: having decisively ended their slump, the Gophers returned to the Rose Bowl the next year and soundly defeated UCLA 21–3.

"Sweet" Home Run Sparks Twins

Killebrew's Blast Conquers Yankees

After six seasons as a starter in the major leagues, Harmon Killebrew was one of the game's most prolific power hitters. Since becoming a regular for the Washington Senators in 1959 at the age of twenty-three, Killebrew had slugged 261 home runs while leading the American League in home runs four times—in 1959, 1962, 1963, and 1964. Of those 261 homers, Killebrew hit 188 during his first four seasons in a Minnesota Twins uniform, after the Senators relocated to Minnesota in 1961.

In 1964, Killebrew hit thirty home runs in the first three months of the season to become just the second player in major-league history to reach that mark before the All-Star Game. (Minnesota native Roger Maris hit thirty-three before the 1961 All-Star break.) Killebrew finished the season with forty-nine home runs and 111 RBIs. In the first half of the 1965 season, he hit sixteen home runs to increase his career total to 288. Number 288 would be one of the most memorable for Killebrew and his teammates.

At the start of the season, the Twins were hoping to show the rest of baseball that their sixth-place finish the previous season was a fluke. After finishing second in 1962 and third in 1963 (winning ninety-one games each season), the Twins had slipped to seventy-nine victories in 1964 despite Killebrew's heroics and a tremendous season by Tony Oliva, who was named the American League rookie of the year. The Twins got off to a good start in 1965, going 27–15 in the first two months. After cooling off a little in June—that month's record 16–13—they sought a strong finish to the first half of the season. They met that goal by winning nine of their first ten games in July. That spurt gave the Twins a 52–29 record and a four-game lead over Cleveland and Baltimore in the A.L. standings heading into their final contest before the All-Star Game—against the defending champion New York Yankees.

Even though the Yankees had been hampered by injuries and were in seventh place with a 41–45 record—thirteen games behind the Twins—they were still the standard by which

Killebrew called his 1965 game-winning home run against the New York Yankees one of his most memorable.

other American League teams were judged. Going into the season, the Yankees had won five consecutive A.L. pennants, giving them twenty-nine in the 44-season span between 1921 and 1964. In the sixteen seasons since 1949, the Yankees had won fourteen league titles.

On Sunday, July 11, a Met Stadium crowd of 35,263 saw the Yankees, sparked by Mickey

Mantle's return to the lineup after a two-week absence, and the Twins battle to a 4–4 tie through eight innings. In the top of the ninth inning, the Yankees broke the tie—after a controversial call prompted Twins manager Sam Mele to continue the game under protest—to take a 5–4 lead into the bottom of the ninth.

Killebrew made Mele's objection moot. He came to the plate against reliever Pete Mikkelsen with two out and a base runner—Rich Rollins, who had walked—at first. Killebrew worked the count to 3-and-2 before fouling off a pitch. He then belted Mikkelsen's next offering 370 feet into the left-field seats for a dramatic two-run home run and a 6–5 victory for the Twins. With this win, the Twins held a five-game lead in the standings. Killebrew, who had beaten the Yankees with a ninth-inning home run off Al Downing the previous year, admitted to the *Minneapolis Tribune* that the home run was "one of the sweeter of the sweet."

Harmon Killebrew played for the Minnesota Twins from 1961 to 1974.

Mele mentioned Killebrew's earlier home run but called this one "more important because you're in a more favorable position at this time, first place." With this momentum, Killebrew and five teammates (Oliva, Earl Battey, Jim Grant, Jimmie Hall, and Zoilo Versalles) appeared in the All-Star Game, which was hosted by the Twins. On Tuesday, July 13, a Metropolitan Stadium crowd of 46,706 watched the National League earn a 6–5 victory. The American League battled back from a 5–0 deficit to tie the score before Ron Santo's single in the seventh inning produced the winning run. But in the memories of Twins fans, Santo's late-inning heroics are overshadowed by those of Killebrew just two days earlier.

October 14, 1965

World Series Comes to Minnesota

Twins and L.A. Dodgers Vie for Title

When the Washington Senators relocated to the Twin Cities prior to the 1961 season, Minnesota acquired a baseball franchise that inspired the quip "Washington—first in war, first in peace and last in the American League." After a seventh-place finish in their first season in Minnesota, the Twins put together back-to-back 90-victory seasons. Retreating to sixth place in 1964, they firmly distanced themselves from their past in 1965.

The Twins went 43–28 in the first three months of the season before heating up in July, when they won ten of their first eleven games to open a five-game lead in the A.L. standings at the All-Star break. The Twins finished July with a 22–9 record, entering the final two months of the season 65–37. They added nineteen wins in August to take eighty-four victories into the final month, surpassing their 1964 total of seventy-nine. On September 26, with five games remaining in the regular season, the Twins clinched the American League pennant with their ninety-ninth victory. They closed out the regular season on October 3 with a 3–2 victory over the California Angels at Metropolitan Stadium. Ending the New York Yankees' string of five consecutive American League pennants, the Twins finished the regular season with a 102–60 record, seven games ahead of the second-place Chicago White Sox.

In the World Series, the Twins met the Los Angeles Dodgers, who had gone 97–65 to win the National League title by two games over the San Francisco Giants. The first two and last two games of the best-of-seven series would be played in Minnesota, while the middle three would be played in Los Angeles. The series opened on October 6 with the Twins beating the Dodgers 8–2 before 47,797 at Metropolitan Stadium. The next day, the Twins took a 2–0 lead in the series behind Jim Kaat, who shut down the Dodgers 5–1 before 48,700 fans.

Shortstop Zoilo Versalles was a key member of the 1965 Minnesota Twins.

**The Minnesota Twins celebrate after defeating the Washington Senators
to clinch the 1965 American League pennant.**

After the series moved to the West Coast, the Dodgers' trio of Claude Osteen, Don Drysdale, and Sandy Koufax limited the Twins to just two runs in three games as the Dodgers won 4–0, 7–2, and 7–0 to take a 3–2 lead.

After a day off, the competition resumed at Metropolitan Stadium. Jim Grant, making his third start of the series, hit a home run and limited the Dodgers to six hits as the Twins

forced a seventh game with a 5–1 victory before 49,578. On Thursday, October 14, a record Metropolitan Stadium crowd of 50,596 showed up to watch a magical game seven.

Dodgers manager Walt Alston, formerly a St. Paul Saints manager, elected to pitch Koufax, who had started game five just three days earlier, choosing him over Drysdale, who was nursing a bone bruise in his pitching hand. After three scoreless innings, the Dodgers managed two runs in the fourth—one a home run by Lou Johnson—off Kaat. The Twins threatened in the bottom of the fifth with runners at first and second and one out, but a great defensive play by third baseman Junior Gilliam rescued Koufax from a jam. The left-handed Koufax got stronger as the game went on, in one stretch, from the fifth to the ninth, retiring twelve consecutive hitters.

After Harmon Killebrew singled with one out in the ninth, Koufax struck out Earl Battey and Bob Allison to end the game, making the Dodgers just the fifth team in history to win the World Series after losing the series' first two games. The three-hit, ten-strikeout performance capped an extraordinary season for Koufax, during which he was 26–8 with a 2.04 ERA and 382 strikeouts in 335 innings. "When I got into the late innings, I could feel I had a lot of strength left," Koufax told the *Minneapolis Tribune*. "I was concerned earlier about pitching on short rest and conserving myself a bit, maybe, but at the finish I never felt better."

Alston was relieved: "It was the toughest decision I've ever had to make, choosing between Drysdale and Koufax."

Twins manager Sam Mele's assessment: "it took the best pitcher in baseball to finally kill us off." Despite the loss, the World Series appearance—the first for the franchise since 1933—transformed a losing legacy.

The NHL and the ABA Arrive in Twin Cities

Beginning in the early 1960s, the Twin Cities area was home to two big-league franchises—the Twins and the Vikings. But in fall 1967, the Minnesota sports scene was significantly altered when the North Stars of the National Hockey League and the Muskies of the American Basketball Association arrived and a new arena, the Metropolitan Sports Center was built. The North Stars and the Muskies shared the new venue, constructed in just twelve months, and made their debuts within twenty-four hours of each other.

The North Stars arrived first. The National Hockey League, which had the same six franchises from 1942 to 1967, announced in February 1966 that the league would double in size, with the expansion franchises beginning play in the 1967–68 season. The Minnesota franchise was awarded to a group whose members included Walter Bush Jr., Gordon Ritz, Wheelock Whitney, Bob Ridder, Harry McNeely, John Ordway Jr., and John Driscoll. They proposed to the league's expansion committee that the team play in the St. Paul Auditorium, but the league insisted on a new building. Eight months after the expansion announcement, ground was broken just north of Metropolitan Stadium in Bloomington for the new arena. A little over two weeks later, the NHL board of governors approved the North Stars' contingency plan to play in the Minneapolis Auditorium if the new arena wasn't ready in time for the start of the 1967–68 season.

On October 11, 1967, the North Stars made their NHL debut, skating to a 2–2 tie in St. Louis against the expansion Blues. Ten days later, after four games on the road (two losses, two ties), the North Stars made their Minnesota debut, playing host to the Oakland Golden Seals, another expansion team. Their first appearance at the Met Center, in front of 12,951 spectators, was a success as Bill Goldsworthy scored the franchise's first "home" goal in the North Stars' 3–1 victory.

The next night, professional basketball returned to Minnesota after a seven-year absence. The Minnesota Muskies got their start in February 1967, when former Minneapolis Laker George Mikan announced the formation of the American Basketball Association. Mikan, who was running a Minneapolis travel agency, had accepted a three-year contract as commissioner of the league, which would be headquartered in Minneapolis. The Minnesota franchise was awarded to California businessman Larry Shields.

After a seven-year absence, professional basketball returned to Minnesota in 1967 with the Minnesota Muskies of the American Basketball Association.

The ABA opened its inaugural season on October 13, and nine days later the Muskies made their Minnesota debut. A Met Center crowd of 8,104 watched the Kentucky Colonels defeat the Muskies 104–96. Louie Dampier, on weekend leave from the National Guard, scored 28 points to pace the Colonels while Sam Smith scored 24 points and Mel Daniels 19 to lead the Muskies.

The crowded sports scene didn't last. While the North Stars quickly became a fixture, the Muskies left town after one season. The next season saw a second ABA franchise, the Pipers, try to make it in Minnesota. But that team bolted after one season as well, leaving the state without a professional basketball team for twenty years [see pages 200–202].

The Los Angeles Kings goalie keeps an eye on the puck during action against the Minnesota North Stars at the Metropolitan Sports Center on November 4, 1967. Two weeks earlier, the North Stars had played their first regular-season home game.

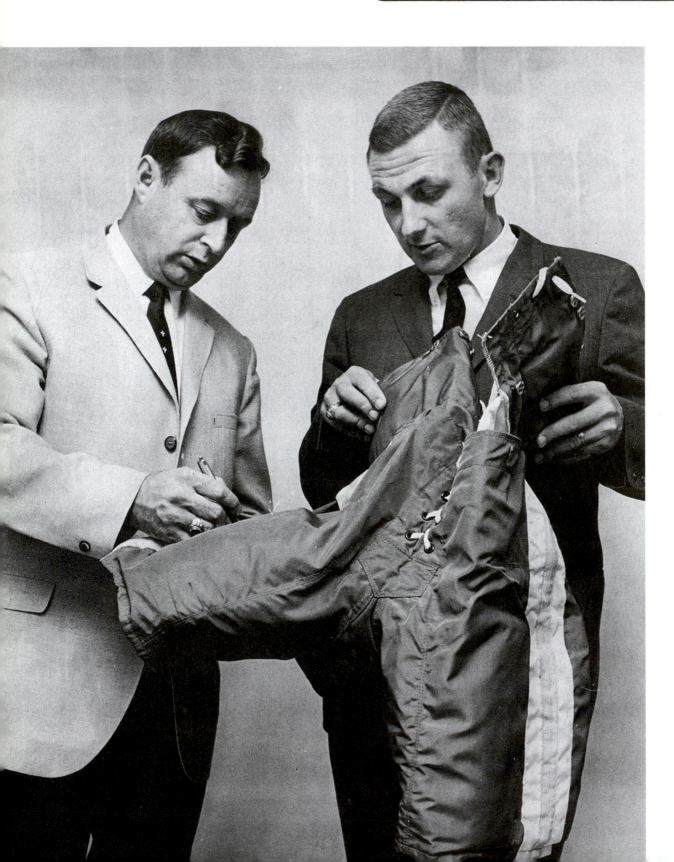

Dream Comes to an End

North Stars Rookie Suffers Fatal Injury

Like many young Canadian hockey players, Bill Masterton hoped to eventually play in the National Hockey League. But Masterton also had a back-up plan. After two seasons of minor league hockey, Masterton returned to school to complete a master's degree in finance in 1963. Then he resumed pursuit of his goal, playing two more seasons in the minors and a season with the U.S. National team. In June 1967, Masterton, a native of Winnipeg, Manitoba, was sold by the Montreal Canadiens to the Minnesota North Stars, becoming the first player under contract to the expansion team.

Four months later, Masterton and the North Stars made their NHL debut in St. Louis. More than six years after earning All-American honors for leading Denver University to the NCAA hockey title, Masterton scored the first goal in franchise history in the North Stars' eventual 2–2 tie with the Blues. Midway through their first season, Masterton and the North Stars had proven their mettle. The twenty-nine-year-old rookie had played in all thirty-eight games for the North Stars, tallying four goals and eight assists to help the North Stars compile a respectable 14–15–8 record and second-place standing in the West Division.

The dream season became a nightmare during the North Stars' next-to-last game before the All-Star break, played at home on Saturday, January 13, against the Oakland Golden Seals. In a game that was described as the "roughest of the season" in the next morning's *Minneapolis Sunday Tribune,* the teams skated to a 2–2 tie. But a collision in the first four minutes rendered the outcome meaningless. Masterton, on his second shift of the game, was apparently checked by an Oakland defenseman after passing the puck. Masterton, like

Bill Masterton, right, was the first player under contract to the expansion Minnesota North Stars. Wren Blair, left, was the North Stars' general manager and coach.

most NHL players of the era, was not wearing a helmet and was knocked unconscious when he hit the ice.

Quickly attended by two doctors, Masterton was taken from the ice on a stretcher and transported to Fairview Southdale Hospital. The account of the game in the *Tribune* said he had sustained undetermined head injuries. The following day's paper reported that, as of late Sunday night, Masterton remained in critical condition, attended by five doctors, two of them neurosurgeons. The newspaper explained that no one was quite certain what had happened on the play. The game had been televised in Oakland, but the incident wasn't shown on camera.

North Stars general manager and coach Wren Blair informed the team—following its 9–2 loss in Boston on Sunday—that Masterton's injuries were so extensive he was not expected to live. He added, "I know that some of you think it was cruel that Bill should die as an athlete when he already had a successful career. But making this team was the greatest achievement of his life, the thing he always wanted to do."

Blair also told the *Minneapolis Tribune* that he wasn't convinced Masterton's death was directly attributable to the blow he had received in the game. He recalled, "Bill was hit in the head during the last few minutes of the Boston game Dec. 30. The players told me he complained for several days afterward of headaches. Looking back on his injury Saturday, I remember that he sort of stood motionless for a moment before falling. I believe he may have had a condition we were not aware of."

At 1:55 A.M. on Monday—thirty hours after being injured and having never regained consciousness—Masterton died. Doctors described the cause of death as "massive brain damage." Masterton, who had left a promising career with Honeywell for a final attempt to reach the NHL, was the first player to die from injuries suffered during a game in the league's fifty-one-year history. He was survived by a wife and two young children.

"When a person dies, it's common to point out his virtues," Blair told the *Minneapolis Tribune*. "In his case, every word you could say would be true. Not only was he an ideal athlete, coachable and blessed with great desire, but one of the finest young men, in every way, that I've been fortunate to meet."

Following the season, the NHL established an award to be given annually to the player who most fits the description "unsung hero." Fittingly, the trophy is named after Bill Masterton.

March 23, 1968
The First to "Three-Peat"

Edina Wins Basketball Title

In the first fifty-five years of the Minnesota boys' state basketball tournament, no school won three consecutive titles. Moorhead had nearly accomplished this feat, winning titles in 1928 and 1929 and reaching the 1930 championship game, only to be defeated by St. Paul Mechanic Arts. Four other schools—Buhl, Minneapolis Henry, Hopkins, and Minneapolis Roosevelt—had managed back-to-back titles. Roosevelt was the last of the five to win consecutive titles, in 1956 and 1957.

So, at the start of the 1967–68 season, the state's basketball fans had two questions about two-time defending champion Edina. The first was whether the Hornets would become the first team in state history to win three consecutive titles. The second was whether the Hornets would go undefeated for a third consecutive season.

The answers were yes and no, respectively.

The Hornets went into the 1967–68 season with the best player in the state—Bob Zender—and a 54-game winning streak. With just three players returning from its 1967 championship team, Edina opened the season with ten wins to move within one of the state record for consecutive victories—sixty-five, set by Hopkins in 1954. On January 26, 1968, the Hornets defeated St. Cloud Tech 65–58 to tie the record, and they broke it four days later, overpowering Cooper 52–34 before twenty-eight hundred in Cooper's gymnasium.

But on February 16, the Hornets' dream of a third consecutive undefeated season evaporated. Playing at home, Richfield defeated the Hornets 81–75 to stop the streak at sixty-nine. The Hornets, trailing by 20 points at halftime and by as many as 25, outscored the Spartans 24–12 to cut their deficit to eight points going into the fourth quarter. Although the Hornets got within six points several times as the clock ran down, the Spartans held on for the victory. The Hornets regrouped to win their next two games, finishing the regular season with

Doug Eha (50) of Highland Park stretches for a rebound at the 1968 state high school tournament, but Moorhead eventually won the game 107–89, setting a scoring record in the process.

a 17–1 mark. The team then earned the District 18 title before defeating Willmar 66–54 for the Region 5 championship.

Edina was joined in the state tournament by two other teams with long winning streaks—Region 1 champion Hayfield, with 25 games, and Region 7 champion Duluth Central, with 23 games. Rounding out the field for the tournament were Mankato (Region 2), Granite Falls (3), St. Paul Highland Park (4), Moorhead (6), and East Grand Forks (8). The latter had finished the regular season with a losing record (8–10) but won five consecutive games to advance to the state tournament. Most observers named Edina as the favorite, but Hornets coach Duane Baglien downplayed his team's chances, telling the *Minneapolis Tribune*'s Ted Peterson, "This looks to me like a repetition of the 1966 tournament with its closeness of competition. Certainly there are three well-matched teams in the upper bracket and the semifinals are going to be terrific no matter who wins."

Edina opened the tournament with a 63–49 victory over Hayfield before a Thursday afternoon crowd of 18,490 at Williams Arena. The Hornets led by just four points early in the fourth quarter before putting the game out of reach with a 10–0 run. Zender scored 17 points and teammate Bill Fiedler added 16.

In the other first-round games, Duluth Central continued to roll with a victory over Granite Falls, and Mankato defeated East Grand Forks. Moorhead's 107–89 victory over

St. Paul Highland Park was a record-breaking performance, topping the tournament scoring record set by Minneapolis Roosevelt's 101 in the 1956 championship game. The combined 196 points by the two teams broke the previous record of 170, set in Bemidji's 91–79 victory over Aurora in the 1956 consolation final.

In Friday's semifinals, Zender went 13-of-17 from the field and scored 35 points as the Hornets stunned Duluth Central 91–61. Moorhead set up a rematch of the 1967 championship game with a 77–57 victory over Mankato.

As they had in their 72–55 victory in 1967, Edina dominated the championship game. The Hornets led by five after the first quarter before outscoring the Spuds 22–9 in the second to open a 36–18 lead at halftime. The Spuds managed to cut the Hornets' lead to fifteen heading into the fourth quarter, but the Hornets outscored them 20–10 over the final eight minutes to pull away for a 70–45 victory. The Hornets limited the Spuds to 31 percent shooting (19-of-62) from the field.

Zender led the Hornets, going 8-of-11 from the field and scoring 19 points. In the three tournament games, he was 29-of-38 (76 percent) from the field and scored 73 points. University of Minnesota basketball coach John Kundla told the *Minneapolis Tribune*'s Sid Hartman that Zender was the best college prospect in the state in ten years. Zender, who had heard from thirty-five colleges, went on to play for the University of Kansas.

The victory capped a 26–1 season and gave the Hornets three titles and a three-season mark of 79–1. Baglien told the *Minneapolis Tribune*, "When you consider this tournament has been running for 56 years,

Bill Fiedler (50) of Edina battles Duluth Central's Jeff Grohs at Williams Arena on March 22, 1968. Edina became the first team in state history to win three consecutive state titles.

and this is the first time one school has won three in a row, you have to salute the kids." Asked to compare the three Edina champions, Baglien replied, "I can't compare teams. Each team has different characteristics. In my book all three have been terrific."

Three years later, the format for the state tournament changed [see pages 134–37], but the Hornets had made their mark as the only team to win three straight titles under the one-class system.

Worth the Wait

Warroad and Henry Boucha Reach State Tournament

With each year, anticipation grew. For nearly five years, Minnesota hockey fans had been hearing about a gifted high school player from the tiny northwestern town of Warroad. Henry Boucha joined the Warroad varsity as an eighth-grader. Two years later he was named all-state, the first sophomore to be so honored. By the time he was a senior he was considered one of the best high school players in state history. Murray Williamson, coach of the 1968 U.S. Olympic Team, told the *Minneapolis Tribune* that Boucha "could easily play for the national team now."

But few fans outside of northwestern Minnesota had seen Boucha and Warroad play. For four consecutive years Warroad had lost to Roseau in the Region 8 tournament.

The 1968–69 season represented Boucha's last chance to play in the state tournament. But again rival Roseau blocked the Warriors' path, edging Warroad 2–1 for the regional championship. Despite the loss—just the fourth in 22 games—the Warriors had another shot at the state tournament thanks to a geographical fluke. The state was divided into eight regions with the top team from each advancing to the state tournament. Because there were no teams in Region 3, the Region 7 and Region 8 runners-up played for that tournament spot.

One night after losing to Roseau, Warroad played Eveleth—winner of five state championships in the first twenty-four years of the state tournament—in Hibbing for the "Region 3" championship. Boucha's reputation grew a little more in the backdoor game. With the score tied late in the second period, Boucha's forehead was cut by an Eveleth player's stick. After receiving medical attention, a determined Boucha, one of his eyes swollen shut, returned to the ice. The teams skated through a scoreless period to end regulation in a 2–2 tie. After one scoreless overtime period, late in the second it appeared the teams were headed for a third extra session. But with one second remaining, Boucha scored to lift the Warriors to a 3–2 victory.

Warroad's Henry Boucha is considered one of the top high school hockey players in state history.

For Boucha and many of his teammates, the trip to the state tournament was only their second to the Twin Cities. Five years earlier, Boucha and the Warroad bantam team had traveled to Wakota Arena in South St. Paul, where they won the state title. Inspiring additional excitement on this trip, the tournament would take place for the first time in the spacious Met Sports Center in Bloomington after being played in the cozy St. Paul Auditorium for years. Drawing eighty thousand spectators, nearly double the previous year's attendance, the tournament was a rare example of an event living up to its hype.

Most of the publicity centered on Greenway of Coleraine, Roseau, and Edina, which were one, two, and three, respectively in the *Minneapolis Tribune*'s pre-tournament state rankings. Coleraine, led by two-time all-stater Mike Antonovich, was seeking its third consecutive state title; Roseau was led by brothers John and Robby Harris; and Edina, making its third consecutive appearance in the tournament, was led by Bill Nyrop. Antonovich and Boucha, who the *Minneapolis Tribune* said had college and pro scouts buzzing, were the players to watch.

In the Warriors' first-round game on Thursday, February 20, they rallied from a 2–0 deficit for a 4–3 victory over Minneapolis Southwest, Boucha's goal early in the third period the eventual game winner. The victory left the Warriors one win shy of the championship game, but they faced their old nemesis—Roseau—in the semifinals. A crowd of 15,066— the largest to attend a high school hockey game in Minnesota—showed up the next night to watch the rematch.

Goals by sophomores Alan Hangsleben and John Taylor put Warroad ahead 2–0 early in the second period, but Roseau sophomore Mike Broten cut the Warriors' lead to 2–1. Seven minutes into the third period, Boucha's unassisted goal restored the Warriors' two-goal advantage. A little over two minutes after Boucha's goal, Broten scored again to make it 3–2, but the Warriors held on to outlast their rivals.

Warroad's opponent in the championship game was Edina, which had routed South St. Paul 7–1 in the other semifinal. On Saturday, February 22, a crowd of 15,063 gathered to see

Warroad's Leo Marshall scores the team's first goal against Edina's Doug Hastings in front of a Met Center crowd of 15,063. Edina needed overtime to defeat Warroad for the 1969 state hockey title.

if Edina could become just the second school from the Twin Cities, following St. Paul Johnson, to win a state hockey title. But most of the crowd was rooting for Warroad.

The Warriors led 2–1 after one period, but the Hornets scored twice in the first two minutes of the second to take a 3–2 lead. A few minutes later, the situation worsened for the Warriors when Boucha was bumped off balance and then checked into the boards by Edina defenseman Jim Knutson. Boucha, who caught an elbow under his jaw, was helped off the ice, and in between periods he was taken to Ramsey County Hospital for x-rays. This time Boucha, who had played all but twenty-four seconds in the tournament prior to the injury, wouldn't return. He remained hospitalized for two days with a ruptured eardrum. Knutson, earning a minor penalty for elbowing, was booed the rest of the night.

Shortly after Boucha left the ice, the Hornets extended their lead to 4–2. But the Warriors, who had just one senior besides Boucha, regrouped, and Frank Krahn scored twice in a two-minute span late in the second period to tie the score. After a scoreless third period, the teams went to overtime, and the game was decided when an unassisted goal by Skip Thomas at 3:09 lifted the Hornets to their first state title.

During the postgame awards ceremony, Boucha's name was announced as a member of the all-tournament team. Even though he wasn't in the building, he was given a standing ovation. In the *Minneapolis Tribune*, reporter John Gilbert called Boucha, "perhaps the single most spectacular player to ever play in the state tournament."

Boucha went on to play for the U.S. Olympic team and spent six seasons in the National Hockey League, but his career was ultimately cut short by injury.

January 11, 1970

Vikings Complete Transition

Former Expansion Team Performs in Super Bowl

The transition from expansion team to league champion happened quickly for the Minnesota Vikings. In the first seven seasons after joining the National Football League in 1961, the Vikings recorded a winning season just once, but the franchise's eighth season saw its fortunes improve. In 1968, under the direction of second-year coach Bud Grant and quarterback Joe Kapp, the Vikings compiled an 8–6 record to earn their first divisional championship. That season ended with a loss to the Baltimore Colts in the first play-off game in team history.

The Vikings went into the 1969 season loaded with experience as nineteen of twenty-two starters from 1968 returned, and the team tuned up for the regular season by winning five of six exhibition games. Their only preseason loss was to the reigning world champion New York Jets, who had upset the Baltimore Colts in the Super Bowl the previous January.

The Vikings opened the regular season with a one-point loss to the New York Giants, a team they had defeated by one point in an exhibition game two weeks earlier. But after their season-opening loss, the Vikings won their next twelve games—the NFL's longest winning streak in thirty-five years. The victories started in week two with a stunning 52–14 defeat of the defending NFL champion Baltimore Colts as Kapp passed for 449 yards and seven touchdowns. Kapp, who in the fourth quarter went to the bench with a sore shoulder, completed 28 of 43 passes, setting team records in both categories, and tied the league record for touchdown passes. The seventh victory was a 51–3 rout of the Cleveland Browns. But the winning streak came to an end in the regular-season finale as the Vikings lost to the Atlanta Falcons in Atlanta, 10–3. Still, the Vikings finished with a league-best record of 12–2.

On December 27, the Vikings played host to a play-off game for the first time in franchise history. Their opponent: the Los Angeles Rams, a team they had defeated 20–13 just three weeks earlier. In the rematch, the Rams led 17–7 at halftime and 20–14 in the fourth

quarter before the Vikings rallied for a 23–20 victory, earning themselves a berth in the NFL championship game. On January 4, 1970, the Vikings scored touchdowns on their first two possessions—the second a 75-yard pass from Kapp to Gene Washington—to take a 14–0 lead over the visiting Cleveland Browns, going on to win the game 27–7. The victory made the Vikings the first "modern" expansion team to win an NFL championship.

The following Sunday, the Vikings and AFL champion Kansas City Chiefs met in New Orleans in Super Bowl IV. The Vikings, who had allowed just 133 points in fourteen regular-season games (9.5 points per game), were installed as 13-point favorites over the Chiefs, who had defeated the Oakland Raiders 17–7 in the AFL championship game. Hoping to become the first world championship team from Minnesota since the Lakers won the 1954 National Basketball Association title, the Vikings dug themselves an early hole in front of a Tulane Stadium crowd of 80,997.

Plus-twelve in turnovers during the regular season, the Vikings committed three mistakes—a dropped pass that would have been a first down and two fumbles—in the first half. The second fumble was the most damaging. After Jan Stenerud's third field goal gave the Chiefs a 9–0 lead with 5:34 remaining in the first half, the Vikings' Charlie West fumbled the ensuing kickoff, which the Chiefs recovered at the Vikings' 19-yard line. Six plays later, Mike Garrett scored on a five-yard run, and Stenerud's extra-point kick made it 16–0. The Vikings managed to pull within nine in the second half, but Otis Taylor's 46-yard touchdown reception put the Chiefs up 23–7, and they sealed the victory with three second-half interceptions.

"All year we won because we didn't make a lot of mistakes," Grant told Sid Hartman of

During his three seasons with the Vikings, quarterback Joe Kapp was protected by future Hall of Famer Ron Yary.

the *Minneapolis Tribune*. "We beat the Rams and the Cleveland Browns without making any mistakes. We made as many against Kansas City as we've made all year. But don't take anything away from the Chiefs. They are one great football team."

The Vikings had committed five turnovers while the Chiefs had just one. Kansas City quarterback Len Dawson completed 12 of 17 passes for 142 yards and a touchdown despite playing on bad knees and being distracted during the week preceding the game by rumors that he was involved in a gambling investigation in Detroit. He was cleared of any involvement but lost a day of preparation.

The loss didn't diminish the fact that the Vikings had become one of the league's dominant teams. They would play in three more Super Bowls in the next seven years.

Carl Eller, who played for the University of Minnesota, was a Viking from 1964 to 1978.

March 21, 1970

Sherburn Wins with Class

Raiders Reign in Final Single-Class Tournament

Talk about ending the one-class state tournament for boys' basketball had been circulating for years. In January 1948, over four hundred superintendents voted by a 2-to-1 margin to split the state tournament into A and B contests. But two months later, the Minnesota State High School League's delegate assembly—one member representing each of the thirty-two districts—voted 27–5 against the proposal. The tournament debate continued into the 1960s. Many of the large Twin Cities high schools thought it unfair that only two teams represented the metropolitan area, home to half the state's population. And some of the smaller schools didn't like having to compete against much bigger schools for a spot in the state tournament. The small schools pointed out that instances like the 1960 tournament—won by tiny Edgerton—proved exceedingly rare [see pages 96–98].

On the eve of the fifty-seventh annual state tournament, the MSHSL was studying four plans for the tournament's future: eliminate regional finals and bring sixteen teams to the tournament; hold separate tournaments for the metropolitan area and for outstate teams; stage A and B tournaments; or keep the tournament one class. The 1970 tournament proved to be a grand finale for the one-class tournament.

Going into regional play, unbeaten Red Wing was considered the favorite to win the state tournament. In the District 3 championship game, Red Wing defeated defending state champion Rochester John Marshall for its twentieth consecutive victory. But the Wingers were stunned by Kenyon in the Region 1 championship game. Coached by Ron Hested, Kenyon trailed by eight going into the fourth quarter but limited the Wingers to three points in the final eight minutes to pull out a 59–57 victory. Red Wing's loss left just one unbeaten team in the state—Sherburn, a small school from south central Minnesota. Hailing from a town of twelve hundred and with a senior class of fifty-four, Sherburn earned its first Region 2 championship with a 48–38 victory over Jackson.

Sherburn's Pete Eiden (50) and Marshall's Brad Rockman go after a rebound during the semifinals of the 1970 state basketball tournament.

With Red Wing on the sidelines, Region 4 champion South St. Paul was the consistent favorite heading into the state tournament. Filling out the field were Marshall (Region 3), Robbinsdale (5), Melrose (6), Eveleth (7), and Park Rapids (8). On March 19, led by Tom Mulso's 29 points, Sherburn opened the tournament with a 65–54 victory over Melrose. Other first-round winners were Marshall (74–63 over Kenyon), South St. Paul (97–61 over Park Rapids), and Robbinsdale (51–35 over Eveleth).

A crowd of 18,435 gathered in Williams Arena on March 20 to watch the semifinals. Jeff McCarron scored 37 points and grabbed 24 rebounds to lead Sherburn to a 71–60 victory over Marshall. In the second semifinal, South St. Paul, with its imposing front line of Brian Peterson (six-foot-six), Mark Stoeve (six-foot-five), and Kurt Virgin (six-foot-two) dominated Robbinsdale, 68–54.

The championship game featured unbeaten Sherburn and South St. Paul, which had lost just once in 26 games. The Raiders won behind a memorable shooting performance by Mulso, as the six-foot-five forward scored 24 points in the first half, helping the Raiders build a 42–29 halftime lead. The Packers closed out the third quarter with a 14–5 run to pull within three points, 54–51, going into the fourth quarter. But the Raiders remained domi-

Sherburn's starting five, (from left) John Tirevold, Paul Krohn, Pete Eiden, Jeff McCarron, and Tom Mulso, pose with their championship trophy in 1970 – the final year there was a single state basketball champion.

nant, outscoring the Packers 24–11 over the final eight minutes. The Packers were led by Virgin, who scored 17 points before fouling out at the start of the fourth quarter. Mulso finished with 39 points in the Raiders' 78–62 victory, and McCarron added 19 points. Mulso, McCarron, and teammate John Tirevold were named to the all-tournament team.

Two months later, on May 22, the MSHSL's board of directors voted unanimously to conduct a two-class tournament—Class AA for the sixty-four largest schools in the state and Class A for the remaining 421 schools—beginning the next season. In a statewide survey, the plan was approved by 78 percent of the superintendents, 75 percent of the principals, 79 percent of the athletic directors, and 80 percent of the coaches. The time had come for a two-class tournament: a recent nationwide survey had reported that forty-three of the forty-eight states that held state tournaments had two or more classes. While twenty-six schools that would play in Class A under the new system had won Minnesota state titles, only six of those had been since 1950. Two of those championships were among the most memorable in state history: the Edgerton Flying Dutchmen in 1960 and the Raiders in 1970.

August 10, 1971

Killebrew Reaches Milestone

Twins Slugger Hits Number 500

Minnesota Twins slugger Harmon Killebrew rarely went very long between home runs. In the Twins' first ten seasons in Minnesota, Killebrew hit 403 home runs in 5,079 at bats—an average of one home run every 12.6 at bats. At the start of the 1971 season, he needed just thirteen home runs to reach the milestone 500, and most observers figured Killebrew would easily attain the standard.

Killebrew hit his eleventh home run of the season—number 498 for his career—on June 22 off Oakland's Daryl Patterson at Met Stadium. Twins officials figured he would soon hit two more, so they planned a promotion for early July to celebrate Killebrew reaching 500. On July 6, a crowd of 26,687 gathered at Met Stadium to honor Killebrew, each fan receiving a commemorative mug. But there were two problems. Bothered by a foot injury, Killebrew sat out the game. And he was still stuck on number 498.

He finally hit number 499 on July 25, off Boston's Luis Tiant in the Twins 6–2 victory over the Red Sox at Met Stadium. In the thirty-three days between Killebrew's 498th and 499th home runs, the Twins had won just nine of twenty-nine games. Two weeks later, Killebrew was still at 499 when the San Francisco Giants came to town for an exhibition game. Prior to the game, Killebrew, ranked number ten on the all-time home run list, and Willie Mays, ranked number two, staged a home-run hitting contest, the start of which was delayed for twenty minutes to accommodate a crowd of 24,719. Mays, who had 643 career home runs, won the contest 6–4, but Killebrew homered in the exhibition game, which was won by the Twins 5–2. The contest and the exhibition proved to be good omens for Killebrew.

Harmon Killebrew opened the 1971 season just thirteen home runs shy of the career milestone 500. He finally hit his 500th homer on August 10.

The next night—August 10—Killebrew stepped to the plate in the bottom of the first inning against Baltimore Orioles lefthander Mike Cuellar and belted the second pitch into the left-field seats to finally reach the milestone. Public address announcer Bob Casey asked the fan who caught the ball to return the souvenir to the dugout, and Bob Hamilton of Golden Valley presented it to Killebrew in exchange for an autographed baseball. The crowd of 15,881 roared.

The wait for home run number 501 wasn't nearly as long. In the sixth inning, Killebrew ripped a two-run home run off Cuellar to tie the game 3–3. But the Orioles went on to win the game on Merv Rettenmund's solo home run in the tenth inning.

After the game, Killebrew admitted to the *Minneapolis Tribune* that he had felt pressure for two weeks from "being asked every day by press, radio and television representatives when I was going to hit No. 500." Twins owner Calvin Griffith told the *Tribune*'s Sid Hartman, "there isn't any question that Harmon was pressing, trying too hard to get No. 500. Now the pressure is off and he seems to have his natural swing back."

Asked if the injury to his right foot—suffered on June 28—had delayed the bid for 500, Killebrew told the *Tribune* he wouldn't use that as an excuse.

Griffith predicted that Killebrew would hit at least a dozen more home runs over the season's final six weeks. He was close: Killebrew slugged fourteen to finish the season with twenty-eight. In the next four years, Killebrew would hit fifty-nine more before retiring in 1975 with 573.

After hitting home run number 500 off Baltimore's Mike Cuellar, Killebrew belted number 501 just five innings later.

January 25, 1972
Basketball Brawl

Gophers and Ohio State Battle for First Place

By 1971, interest in the University of Minnesota men's basketball program was waning. The Gophers had managed just four winning seasons since 1957, and during that period there were just two seasons when their attendance averaged more than ten thousand fans per game.

Bill Musselman turned the team around in his first season as the Gophers' coach although, ironically, he hadn't been Minnesota's first choice in April 1971. Murray State coach Cal Luther had verbally accepted an offer to become the third new Gopher coach in four seasons but then changed his mind forty-eight hours later. The next day—April 5—the thirty-year-old Musselman accepted a four-year contract to coach for Minnesota. Despite his age, Musselman had already been a college head coach for six seasons, directing Ashland (Ohio) College to a 129–30 record. Ashland's 1968–69 team had set an NCAA record by allowing just 33.9 points per game. In addition to being successful, Musselman's teams were entertaining. Ashland had gained nationwide notoriety for its pregame warm-up drills, which displayed Harlem Globetrotters–style ball handling.

In Musselman's first season with the Gophers, their victories and the entertaining pregames quickly caught the attention of basketball fans. After going 4–3 in their first seven games, the Gophers won their final two nonconference games to take a 6–3 record into the Big Ten portion of their schedule. On January 8, 1972, they opened their conference schedule by playing host to Indiana and its new coach Bob Knight. In front of 19,121—the second-largest crowd in Williams Arena history—the Gophers pulled out a 52–51 win. They followed up with victories over Northwestern (84–60), Wisconsin (65–59), and Michigan State (67–57) to improve their conference record to 4–0, their best start in conference play since they had opened the 1948–49 season with five consecutive victories.

The undefeated start in conference play made the next game for the Gophers—at home against unbeaten Ohio State—one of the most anticipated Big Ten games in school history. Ohio State, which had won seven conference titles in the previous thirteen seasons, brought a 3–0 conference record into the contest. Musselman told the *Minneapolis Tribune* that the game was more important than any other he had been involved with: "I've had teams play in the college division play-offs, and those were mighty important games. But this one is more important because it could lead to a Big Ten championship. It's very important because it's the only time we play Ohio State and they are the team to beat in the conference. We have to do it ourselves."

The teams displayed contrasting styles. The Buckeyes and guard Allan Hornyak, who led the conference in scoring with 29.7 points per game, were averaging a conference-best 80.5 points per game. The Gophers, who hadn't won a conference title in thirty-five years, were leading the Big Ten in defense, allowing just 56.5 points per game.

A capacity crowd of 17,775 witnessed the most-debated Gopher basketball game ever. The teams played to a 23–23 tie at halftime, and the Gophers led by one point, 32–31, with 11:25 remaining when the Buckeyes took control. Over the next six minutes, the Buckeyes held the Gophers scoreless while using a 9–0 run to open a 40–32 lead. After the Gophers managed to pull within six with less than a minute left in the game, the Buckeyes brought the ball down the floor. With thirty-six seconds remaining, Buckeyes center Luke Witte was fouled and knocked to the floor by the Gophers' Clyde Turner. The officials ruled Turner's foul flagrant, and he was ejected from the game. But before Turner left the floor, a brawl erupted. Both benches emptied and some spectators joined the melee on the Williams Arena's elevated playing surface. It took at least twenty minutes to restore order.

The brawl sent three Buckeyes to a hospital and ended the game. Mark Minor was treated for cuts and released. Mark Wagar, who suffered lacerations over his left eye, and Witte, who suffered deep cuts over his chin and eyebrow, were kept overnight for observation. After the game, representatives from both teams debated what started the brawl: "Clyde told me he swung his arm to block the shot," Musselman told the *Minneapolis Tribune*. "He said that's all he did. Then Corky [Taylor] went over to help Witte up and he said Witte spit at him. I wasn't close enough to see what happened and I don't know who did what. But when a game is played with this much emotion you've got to start calling them as close as you can the first time a guy takes a swing."

The game had been physical and intense from the opening tip-off. "I know that [Ohio State coach] Fred Taylor will take a shot at our pregame warm-up," Musselman said, "but I

The Gophers and the Buckeyes were both unbeaten in Big Ten play going into their 1972 showdown at Williams Arena. A crowd of 17,775 watched Bob Nix and two Ohio State players go after a loose ball in the first half.

Luke Witte (34) suffered facial lacerations in the brawl that halted the game with just thirty-six seconds remaining. The Gophers' Ron Behagen (11) was suspended for his actions in the game's final minute.

see our point man, Bob Nix, get hammered all night by Hornyak and nothing is called. And when Witte picks out the smallest guy [Nix] and fires an elbow at him [as the teams were leaving the floor at the end of the first half] and nothing is called . . ."

Hornyak told the *Minneapolis Tribune* that he and his teammates "could feel the tension right from the start of the game. As long as Minnesota was in the game, nothing happened. But once we got in front eight points, Turner, Jim Brewer and others on the Minnesota team just seemed to explode and lose their head."

Fred Taylor and his athletic director, Ed Weaver, told the *Minneapolis Tribune* that the Gophers' pregame show sparked the capacity crowd. "If it's that important to their well-being," Taylor commented, "why don't they do it on the road. Think about that for a minute."

The brawl had been witnessed by Big Ten commissioner Wayne Duke and was featured nationally in a two-page spread in the next issue of *Sports Illustrated*. "We plan to review the game with the officials," Duke told the *Minneapolis Tribune*. "We will be talking to the coaches and athletic directors at both schools. We want to make sure we will never have a repetition of anything like this. In all my years in sports, I've never seen anything like this develop before. It was most embarrassing. We'll make sure it doesn't happen again."

Three days later, Corky Taylor and Ron Behagen, who had joined the brawl even though he had fouled out of the game midway through the second half, were suspended by the Big Ten for the remainder of the season. Behagen's spot in the Gophers' starting lineup was filled by Dave Winfield. The Gophers—behind Winfield, Turner, Brewer, Nix, and Keith Young—regrouped and won seven of their last nine games to earn the conference title—the school's first outright title since 1919—and the school's first NCAA tournament appearance. The season, though marred by the brawl, succeeded in sparking renewed interest in the program.

November 17, 1972

No More "Mythical" Champions

Football Play-off Format Unveiled

For the first sixty years that high school football was played in Minnesota, there was no official state champion. But as early as 1911 a "mythical" champion was named: that year's was Litchfield, with team member Bernie Bierman, future University of Minnesota coach. Starting in 1947, Ted Peterson of the *Minneapolis Tribune* picked a state champion at the end of each season. Not long after, observers began discussing a play-off format to determine the true state champion, and, finally, in 1972 a play-off system was unveiled. The 477 schools in the state were split into five classes—AA, A, B, C, and 9-man—with the top four teams in each class advancing to the play-offs. The Minnesota State High School League determined the play-off teams by recording points: one hundred for each victory and fifty for each tie, plus bonus points for victories by teams defeated.

At the start of the 1972 season, there were two teams to watch in Class AA—Moorhead and Minneapolis Washburn. Moorhead, the "mythical" champion in 1971, opened the season with a 40–6 win over Fargo (North Dakota) South. The victory was the eighteenth consecutive—thirty-ninth in the previous 41 games—for the Spuds. Minneapolis Washburn also had a long winning streak. On October 13, the Millers defeated Minneapolis Southwest 13–0 at Parade Stadium for their fortieth consecutive victory, extending their unbeaten streak to 55 games. Four weeks later, the Millers defeated previously unbeaten St. Paul Harding 21–6 in the Twin City Championship game at Memorial Stadium, the eighteenth consecutive year a Minneapolis school reigned victorious in the series between the two cities.

The following week, the play-off teams were announced, and in Class AA Moorhead and Minneapolis Washburn were joined by Richfield and Hastings. In the semifinals on November 10, Washburn defeated Richfield 27–7 before twelve thousand at Parade Stadium, its forty-fifth consecutive victory. The next night, the Spuds defeated Hastings 17–7 before eight thousand for their twenty-sixth consecutive victory. Then, on November 17 Washburn and

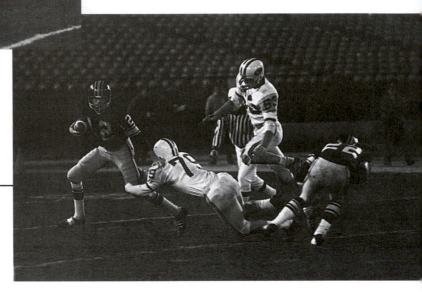

Burnsville's George Harris (87) fights for a pass in the 1972 Class A championship football game versus Sauk Centre. Burnsville claimed the title, 46–19.

Burnsville quarterback Mark Jaeger (12) is stopped by Sauk Centre's Larry Hittle (79) in the 1972 Class A title game at Metropolitan Stadium.

Moorhead, ranked in the *Minneapolis Tribune*'s poll as number one and number two, respectively, met at Metropolitan Stadium for the state championship.

Washburn struck early with two first-quarter touchdowns to take a 14–0 lead. The Millers extended their lead to 20–0 in the second quarter on Steve Sagedahl's second touchdown pass, and Ross Baglien's third touchdown of the game gave the Millers a 26–0 lead in the fourth quarter. The Spuds managed a late touchdown, but the Millers won, 26–8. The victory—before a crowd of about sixteen thousand—was the forty-sixth consecutive for the Millers, stretching their unbeaten streak to 60 games, both marks state records. The loss was just the third in 51 games for the Spuds.

The other inaugural state champions were Burnsville (Class A), Mountain Iron (B), Gaylord (C), and Rothsay (9-man). Rothsay had extended its winning streak to 25 games with a 64–12 victory over Cotton in the 9-man championship game.

While there was the issue that several unbeaten teams—Eden Prairie (Class A), Mahnomen (B), Elmore and Lamberton (C), and Wilson (9-man)—did not make the play-offs, the new format was generally well received, making "mythical" champions a thing of the past.

March 16, 1974
Brooks Revives Program

Gophers Claim NCAA Hockey Title

In spring 1971, the University of Minnesota hockey team finished second at the NCAA Final Four. The Gophers followed up their championship game appearance with three consecutive losing seasons, the first streak of that length in the program's fifty-two years. The first season following the runner-up finish was especially painful: an 8–24 record, the most losses in school history. Herb Brooks, a Gopher for three seasons (1956–59) and member of two U.S. Olympic teams (1964 and 1968), was hired in 1972 to restore the program.

The Gophers showed improvement almost immediately, going 15–14–3 in the 1972–73 regular season before two losses to Wisconsin in the Western Collegiate Hockey Association play-offs. They opened the 1973–74 season by going winless in their first five games, starting with a 4–3 loss at Minnesota-Duluth, followed by two losses to Wisconsin at home before a tie and loss to Michigan at home. Far from humiliating, three of the four losses were by one goal. The Gophers rallied to put an end to their losing streak, going unbeaten in their next nine games, improving to 8–4–2 and outscoring their opponents 53–30 in that stretch. The Gophers went 9–6–3 over their next eighteen games before closing out the regular season with back-to-back losses (5–1 and 4–2) at top-ranked Michigan Tech. Minnesota finished second in the WCHA with a 14–9–5 record.

In the opening round of the WCHA play-offs, the Gophers, who had lost only two of their final sixteen regular-season home games, swept Michigan 5–1 and 5–4. The next weekend, the Gophers tied Denver 3–3 before defeating the Pioneers 2–1 in a second game, earning the WCHA play-off championship and a trip to the NCAA Final Four in Boston.

In the Final Four semifinals on March 14, the Gophers grabbed an early 3–0 lead against

The 1973–74 Gopher hockey team earned the first NCAA title in school history. The championship was the first of three under coach Herb Brooks.

Boston University, but the hometown Terriers roared back to tie the game, 4–4. With less than a minute left in regulation, the Terriers went on the power play. But with just thirteen seconds remaining, Mike Polich, who led the Gophers in scoring with 52 points (19 goals, 33 assists), poked the puck free and fired a 35-foot shot past Terriers goalie Ed Walsh to lift the Gophers to a 5–4 victory.

This win earned the Gophers a rematch with Michigan Tech, which had defeated Harvard in overtime in the other semifinal. Late in the first period of the championship game, John Sheridan scored to give the Gophers a 1–0 lead, and early in the second period John

Perpich made it 2–0. A goal by Michigan Tech's George Lyle trimmed the Gophers' lead to 2–1, but Robby Harris restored the two-goal lead at 4:45 of the third period. Two minutes later, Pat Phippen made it 4–1. The Huskies scored in the final minute but it wasn't enough as the Gophers won 4–2, earning their first NCAA hockey title.

The Huskies had outshot the Gophers 36–27, but Brad Shelstad made thirty-four saves for the Gophers. He was named the goalie on the six-player all-tournament team and the tournament's most outstanding player. Ironically, Shelstad had been left off the All-American team, announced the previous day, and the Gophers were the only team of the four semifinalists not represented. "Our club hasn't been interested in individual honors," Brooks told the *Minneapolis Tribune*. "But Brad deserves every award they can give."

A few months after the championship game, Brooks recalled the night for the *Tribune:* "After that title game was over, I was emotionally drained. I didn't even go into our locker room. That was the kids' achievement. I went to the quietest corner of the [Boston] Garden and found an old beer case and sat down."

The Gophers, who had been named co-national champions in 1929 and the national AAU champions in 1940, had made four previous trips to the NCAA Final Four, where they finished second three times (1953, 1954, and 1971) and third once (1961). With their 1974 victory, the Gophers became the first team in twenty-five years to win the national title with a roster made up solely of Americans. Brooks further embellished the program's newly restored luster by coaching the Gophers to NCAA titles in 1976 and 1979.

Herb Brooks, who played for the University of Minnesota from 1956 to 1959, led the Gophers to an NCAA title in his second season as coach.

December 28, 1975

A Wing and a Prayer

Cowboys' Hail Mary Pass Stuns Vikings

In the seven seasons between 1968 and 1974, the Minnesota Vikings won six division titles and played in the Super Bowl three times. At the start of the 1975 season, they were looking for their third consecutive National Football Conference championship, and many observers thought that the 1975 team would accomplish what none of the previous six division champions had: a Super Bowl win. But the Vikings fell thirty seconds and one miracle short of a return trip to the NFC championship game.

Fielding future Hall of Famers Paul Krause, Alan Page, Fran Tarkenton, and Ron Yary, the Vikings opened the 1975 season by winning ten consecutive games. Then a loss by the second-place Detroit Lions on Thanksgiving Day clinched their seventh division title in eight seasons. Despite two losses in their final four regular-season games, the Vikings finished with the league's best record—a 12–2 mark that made them 84–28 since 1968.

Eight days after closing out the regular season with a 35–13 victory at Buffalo, the Vikings played host to the Dallas Cowboys in an NFC divisional play-off game. The Cowboys had astonished some observers during the regular season by compiling a 10–4 record despite starting twelve rookies. Home-field advantage and a solid defense, which had allowed fewer than 13 points per game, were expected to propel the Vikings into the NFC championship game. But Vikings coach Bud Grant didn't underestimate the Cowboys. "Some people were surprised that Dallas eventually made it to the playoffs," Grant told the *Minneapolis Tribune*. "I wasn't. I saw them as contenders after we played them in the exhibition season." The Vikings had defeated the Cowboys 16–13 in a preseason match-up in Dallas, but the teams hadn't met during the regular season.

With a slight chance of snow and temperatures in the twenties with light winds, the weather wasn't expected to be a factor in the December 28 contest. For most of the game, the defenses were in control. The only touchdown of the first half resulted from a fluke mistake

Dallas Cowboys receiver Drew Pearson and Vikings defensive back Nate Wright fight for the ball at the 5-yard line while Vikings defensive back Paul Krause (22) watches the miracle pass that sealed the Cowboys' victory.

by the Cowboys. Early in the second quarter, the Vikings' Fred McNeill recovered a punt at the Cowboys' 4-yard line after the rolling ball was accidentally touched by one of the Cowboys. Three plays later, Chuck Foreman dove over from the 1-yard line, and Fred Cox's extra-point kick gave the Vikings a 7–0 lead.

The Cowboys tied the score midway through the third quarter with a nine-play, 72-yard drive and then took a 10–7 lead on Toni Fritsch's 29-yard field goal on the first play of the fourth quarter. Midway through the quarter, the Vikings finally put together a scoring drive. Brent McClanahan's one-yard touchdown run—which capped an eleven-play, 70-yard drive—and Cox's extra point put the Vikings ahead 14–10 with 5:46 remaining. Soon, with a minute to go in the game, fans started to relax as it appeared the Vikings would hold on.

Then came the miracle play. On a fourth-and-sixteen situation from the Cowboys' 25-yard line, Roger Staubach completed a pass to Drew Pearson at midfield. Pearson made a leaping catch at the 50 near the sideline but appeared to come down with the catch out-of-bounds. An official ruled that Vikings defensive back Nate Wright hit Pearson in mid-air, forcing him out-of-bounds. The drive still alive, the Cowboys had one more chance. Pearson streaked down the sideline while Staubach lofted a pass toward him from midfield, and, despite contact with Wright, Pearson managed to catch the ball at the Vikings' 5-yard line and go in for a touchdown with twenty-four seconds remaining.

Staubach later admitted, "I just threw it and prayed. I couldn't see whether or not Drew had caught it. I didn't know we had the touchdown, until I saw the official raise his arms."

Quarterback Fran Tarkenton was one of four future Hall of Famers on the 1975 Vikings team.

The play stunned the Metropolitan Stadium crowd of 46,425, many of whom thought Pearson had pushed Wright to get to the ball. But no penalty was called. "From our side of the field," Grant told the *Minneapolis Tribune*, "there is no question Nate was pushed. No question. [Pearson] had nothing to lose. If they called a penalty on him, what had they lost? They would just line up and throw another long pass. Any other type of game—a clear-cut decision, a lopsided loss—would have been easier to take than this. It's things out of our control that we feel most frustrated about."

The bewildered fans quickly recovered, venting their frustration in the game's final half-minute. One fan threw a whiskey bottle onto the field, knocking down official Armen Terz-

Fred Cox, the Vikings' placekicker from 1963 to 1977, is the team's all-time leading scorer.

ian. "I had just picked up one bottle and thrown it off the field," Terzian told the *Tribune*. "I wasn't expecting another." Terzian, who wasn't involved in the controversial touchdown, suffered a deep gash on his forehead. After the game, Vikings president Max Winter offered a five thousand dollar reward for information leading to the bottle-thrower's arrest. Grant regretted the incident, saying, "A terrible, terrible thing. I want to apologize to [Terzian] and to the whole country."

Shortly after the game, quarterback Tarkenton was informed that his father, Reverend Dallas Tarkenton, had suffered a fatal heart attack while watching the match on television.

The Cowboys went on to the Super Bowl, where they lost to the Pittsburgh Steelers. It was the second straight Super Bowl title for the Steelers, who had beaten the Vikings the previous year. The Vikings recovered the next season, reaching the Super Bowl for a fourth time.

First "Official" Girls' State Tournament

The story behind the inaugural "official" girls' state basketball tournament is one of three eras. The initial era covers the first four decades of the twentieth century, when girls' high school basketball was prominent throughout Minnesota, until 1939, when it disappeared statewide [see pages 14–18]. The second begins in 1969, when the Minnesota State High School League officially adopted girls' sports. For the ensuing five years, there was no statewide season set for either girls' basketball or girls' volleyball, so schools were free to choose which season—fall or winter—to play each sport.

In 1974, the MSHSL established a fall season for volleyball, conducting the first state volleyball tournament (won by Osseo) in November of that year. The move to make volleyball a fall sport—and basketball a winter one—wasn't greeted with unanimous support. *Minneapolis Tribune* sportswriter Bruce Brothers reported that a Wadena radio station surveyed sixty-eight athletic directors in Region 6 (which included Alexandria, Brainerd, Little Falls, and Moorhead), finding that sixty-five favored keeping girls' basketball in the fall while one preferred the winter and two were undecided.

Dorothy McIntyre of the MSHSL explained the league's decision, noting that the number of schools with girls' basketball teams had grown from 160 in 1972 to about 220 in 1973 and to 407 at last count. "You set objectives for the overall program and our aim is to bring programs together so we have a fall team sport and a winter team sport for girls," McIntyre said. "There are more than 300 schools in our girls' volleyball program now, even though many are competing against fall basketball at their schools. Obviously one [sport] must be during the fall and one during the winter."

As a transition, there were two basketball seasons during the 1974–75 school year, and each season had its own play-off. In November 1974, eight schools out of 220 gathered in St. Cloud for the fall play-offs, where Glencoe completed a perfect 21–0 season with a 46–29 victory over Wadena in the championship game. Three months later, a winter play-off was held, and Holy Angels defeated Le Sueur 39–37 for the championship. In spring 1975, the MSHSL board of directors voted unanimously to treat girls' basketball as a "winter" activity. This decision opened the modern era of the championship tournament saga.

In February 1976, the first "official" tournament was held, with champions determined in two classes. The eight-team Class A field included Edgerton Southwest Christian, Esko, Glencoe, Mahnomen, Marshall-University, Redwood Falls, Rochester Lourdes, and Starbuck while the Class AA field included Austin, Benilde–St. Margaret's, Bloomington Jefferson, Hibbing, Hill-Murray, St. Paul Central, Wadena, and Worthington. St. Paul Central, led by Linda Roberts and Lisa Lissimore, defeated Wadena and Austin to reach the Class AA championship game. Benilde–St. Margaret's came to the championship game with a 41–29 victory over Hill-Murray.

On February 22, a crowd of 10,054 gathered at the Met Sports Center in Bloomington to watch the championship game. During the regular season, Benilde–St. Margaret's had edged St. Paul Central by two points, 49–47. The rematch was just as close. Benilde–St. Margaret's led by three going into the fourth quarter, but the Minutemaids used a 12–4 run to open a 46–41 lead with 1:22 remaining, and St. Paul Central held on for a 49–47 victory. Improving their record to 17–3 and led by

St. Paul Central's Debbie Krengal drives to the basket against Wadena in the first round of the 1976 Class AA girls' state basketball tournament. Central defeated Wadena en route to the championship.

Steph Torgerson (43) of Glencoe tries to throw off opponent Joan Hopfenspirger's shot as Glencoe and Marshall-University battle in the semifinals of the 1976 Class A girls' basketball tournament at the Met Center.

Roberts's 17 rebounds, St. Paul Central had a decisive 46–16 rebound advantage. The loss was the first in 21 games for Benilde–St. Margaret's.

In Class A, Glencoe, the 1974 fall play-offs winner, reached the championship game with a 58–34 victory over Mahnomen and a 53–51 semifinal victory over Marshall-University. Redwood Falls advanced to the championship game with a 55–42 victory over Rochester Lourdes and a 62–30 victory over unbeaten Edgerton Southwest Christian. Redwood Falls defeated Glencoe 41–28 for the title. Pam Wittwer scored 15 points for Redwood Falls.

The 1976 state tournament showed how quickly girls' basketball was re-introduced statewide.

June 9, 1976

Immortal Visits Minnesota

Minnesota Kicks Face Pelé

The world's game came to Minnesota in May 1976, and it quickly became a social phenomenon. The state's first professional soccer game had to be delayed fifteen minutes to accommodate the crowd waiting to purchase tickets. To speed things along, the owners of the Minnesota Kicks let two thousand fans enter the stadium for free. Over twenty thousand saw the Kicks win their debut in Minnesota, 4–1 over the San Jose Earthquakes.

One month later, the Kicks set a North American Soccer League attendance record when they played host to the New York Cosmos. The star player of the Cosmos was arguably the world's best-known athlete, as Larry Batson of the *Minneapolis Tribune* confirmed: "there are stars in soccer. There are a handful of immortals. Then there is Pelé alone above them all."

Pelé had led Brazil to three World Cup titles—the first at age seventeen. During a professional career that began when he was sixteen, Pelé had scored 1,246 goals in 1,295 games. Putting Pelé's fame in perspective, Batson wrote: "On Nov. 19, 1969, two American astronauts landed on the moon. That was, in much of the world, the second-most important story of the day. For, that same day, in Rio de Janeiro, Pelé scored his 1,000th goal." Professional soccer player Kyle Rote Jr. told Batson, "Once seen, Pelé can never be forgotten. He is a creator, a genius." Pelé had also been termed a missionary and a demigod, and, as Batson related, "the pope reportedly said when Pelé confessed that he was nervous about meeting him: 'me, too.'"

Prior to their appearance in Minnesota, the Cosmos and Pelé drew fifty-eight thousand spectators for an exhibition in Seattle. Four days before the Kicks game, the Cosmos played

A chance to see Brazilian soccer legend Pelé attracted more than forty-six thousand people to Metropolitan Stadium in 1976.

before an NASL regular-season record 42,611 fans in Tampa, Florida. In Minnesota, a crowd of 46,164—with many attending their first soccer game—packed Metropolitan Stadium to pay homage to Pelé. The game was scoreless for sixty-seven minutes before the Kicks' Ace Ntsolengue scored. Four minutes after Ntsolengue's goal, Pelé assisted on Georgio Chinaglia's game-tying goal. With eleven minutes remaining, Tony Field scored to give the Cosmos a 2–1 victory.

Kicks coach Fred Goodwin told the *Minneapolis Tribune,* "It was a marvelous crowd. We're a lot better than we showed. We played too casually in the first half. [Pelé] is still clever enough to nudge them off the ball."

There were other memorable moments for the Kicks during their first season in Minnesota. In late July, nearly thirty-one thousand showed up at the Met to see the Kicks defeat San Diego 4–0. On August 13, the Kicks concluded the regular season with a 1–0 victory in San Diego. Ade Coker scored for the Kicks, who won nine of their final ten regular-season games to lead their division with a 15–9 record. On August 21, the Kicks won their play-off opener 3–0 over Seattle before a NASL play-off record crowd of 41,405 at Metropolitan Stadium. Four days later, the Kicks defeated San Jose 3–1 before another record home crowd of 49,572, earning a spot in the NASL championship game. The Kicks' remarkable season ended with a 3–0 loss to Toronto before 25,765 in Seattle.

The Kicks would enjoy tremendous success in their first four seasons in Minnesota, winning a division title each year. But they quickly vanished from the scene when the NASL folded the franchise in 1981.

Freshman Janet Karvonen Leads Eagles to Title

In February 1976, over thirty-four thousand fans witnessed the first girls' state high school basketball tournament. The *Minneapolis Tribune* reported that attendees "thought it was a good show for the prices." Those gathered for the second state tournament likely had a favorable impression as well—thanks to a fourteen-year-old freshman and her teammates. For many fans, the 1977 state tournament provided the first glimpse of Janet Karvonen and the stellar New York Mills team. It wouldn't be the last.

Starting a senior, junior, sophomore, and eighth grader in addition to Karvonen, New York Mills brought a 22–1 record into the state tournament. A five-foot-ten forward, Karvonen averaged 19 points per game during the regular season for the Eagles, whose per-game team average was 72 points. In one regular-season game, the Eagles defeated Parkers Prairie 129–15.

The Eagles were nearly flawless in their 68–43 victory over Buhl in the first round of the state tournament. A Met Center crowd of 4,425 watched them sink their first seven shots en route to a 14–4 lead. By halftime, the Eagles had extended that lead to 24 points, leaving the court with the score at 42–18. They missed just four field-goal attempts in the first half, shooting 83 percent (20-of-24), and for the game they shot 64 percent (30-of-47). Karvonen contributed by going 14-of-16 (88 percent) from the field and scoring 29 points—two girls' state tournament records. (Jayne Mackley of Hibbing had scored 27 points in the Class AA quarterfinals just the day before). In addition to Karvonen's two marks, the Eagles set four team tournament records in the victory: points (68), field goals (30), field-goal percentage (63.8), and points in one quarter (22).

Freshman Janet Karvonen led New York Mills to the first of three consecutive girls' state basketball championships in 1977.

In the next day's semifinals, New York Mills survived with defense. After trailing Marshall-University 22–18 at halftime, the Eagles rallied for a 48–32 victory. With two minutes left in the third quarter, Marshall-University was leading 29–24, but the Eagles outscored the Cardinals 24–3 over the game's final ten minutes, limiting the Cardinals to just two field goals in the second half and none in the fourth quarter. Karvonen had 15 points and 18 rebounds, and sophomore Jenny Miller contributed 14 points and 12 rebounds.

In the other Class A semifinal, Mayer Lutheran rallied for a 42–40 victory over Heron Lake. It was the first loss for Heron Lake, which had defeated defending state champion Redwood Falls 42–38 in the quarterfinals.

The Class A championship on March 26 went down to the wire. Mayer Lutheran, which led 24–20 at halftime, scored the first four points of the second half to open an eight-point lead. But the Eagles narrowed the margin to four points going into the fourth quarter and then, with a rebound basket by junior Tina Rutten, took their first lead, 37–35, with 4:50 remaining. Less than two minutes later, Rutten's rebound basket and free throw put the Eagles ahead 40–37. With less than three minutes left in the game, Mayer Lutheran pulled within one on a basket by Cindy Balzum. The Eagles went into a stall but lost possession of the ball with thirty-seven seconds remaining. Rutten rebounded a Mayer Lutheran miss to give the Eagles the ball back, and then the Eagles ran out the clock for the victory.

Karvonen had 15 points to finish with a three-game tournament total of 59, breaking the tournament record of 53 set the previous year by Isabella Ceplecha of Redwood Falls. Karvonen also set tournament records for field goals (26), rebounds (44), and field-goal percentage (61.9). For Eagles coach Kathy Lervold, the championship was an early wedding gift. Lervold had announced her engagement on Valentine's Day, telling the team that all she wanted for a wedding present was a state championship. Lervold explained to the *Minneapolis Tribune* that by winning the championship the Eagles met their lofty goal: "We posted an 'unreachable star' at the top of our bulletin board in the locker room at school and that was our goal. We reached it tonight." The state championship was the first of three consecutive for the Eagles. In Karvonen's senior year (1980), the Eagles lost to Austin Pacelli in the semifinals of the state tournament.

During her New York Mills career, Karvonen scored 3,129 points, becoming the first high school player in state history to reach 3,000 points and surpassing the boys' record of 2,852 set by Foley's Norm Grow. Karvonen, who went on to play at Old Dominion and Louisiana Tech, was selected as the U.S. girls high school player of the year as a senior. She was eventually named to the National High School Hall of Fame, Minnesota Sports Hall of Fame, and Minnesota High School Hall of Fame. Following her playing career, Karvonen continued to be a role model by serving as a television commentator and by managing basketball camps for girls.

New York Mills defeated Marshall-University in the semifinals to advance to the 1977 Class A championship game. Tina Rutten, left, scored a key basket in the next day's game against Mayer Lutheran.

Carew Steals Spotlight

Twins Infielder Makes a Run at .400

After winning back-to-back American League West titles in 1969 and 1970, the Minnesota Twins endured some lean times, generating just two winning seasons, 1974 and 1976, in the next six years. Although they drew 2.6 million fans in 1969 and 1970, the Twins averaged just 793,535 spectators per season between 1971 and 1976. But fans returned to Met Stadium in the summer of 1977, having glimpsed things to come the year before, when the Twins went 85–77 in their first season under Gene Mauch to finish third in the A.L. West—just five games behind first-place Kansas City. Fueling the Twins' resurgence was Rod Carew, who had won five league batting titles, including four straight from 1972 to 1975, and had a lifetime batting average of .328 going into the 1977 season.

In late June, the Chicago White Sox came to town for a series between the division contenders, and on June 25 they defeated the Twins 8–1 to move past them into first place. Carew was 1-for-3 before leaving the game in the seventh inning with chest pains, but upon examination he was cleared to play the next day. The contest on Sunday, June 26—"Jersey Day" at Met Stadium—prompted Mauch, who had played nine years in the major leagues and was in his eighteenth season as a major-league manager, to say, "I've never had a game like this. Nothing even close."

It's likely the Met Stadium crowd of 46,963—a Twins' record for a regular-season game—agreed with Mauch. The game was unforgettable from the start, as the first four innings took more than two hours to play and the teams combined for twenty-five runs, the Twins leading 15–10. Twins right fielder Glenn Adams drove in seven runs in the first three

Two Minnesota legends – Rod Carew and Sid Hartman – talk before a game at Metropolitan Stadium.

Rod Carew earned his sixth American League batting title in 1977 with a .388 average, the highest batting average in twenty years.

innings—doubling in two in the first, driving in four in the second with his first career grand slam, and singling in one in the third. He added his team-record eighth RBI with a sacrifice fly in the seventh inning and finished with four hits to raise his batting average to .357.

But the day's standout player was Carew. After he doubled in his first at bat and singled in the second inning, his updated batting average—.400—was posted on the scoreboard, prompting the crowd to give Carew a standing ovation. He singled again in the fourth inning to raise his average to .401 and inspire another ovation. Carew walked and scored in the seventh inning as the Twins extended their lead to 17–10, and he finished the day in style, hitting a two-run home run in the bottom of the eighth and giving the Twins a 19–10 lead. The White Sox scored two runs in the ninth inning, but the Twins moved back into first place with a 19–12 victory.

For the day, Carew was 4-for-5—raising his batting average to .403—with a career-high six RBIs. "The ovations gave me butterflies," Carew told the *Minneapolis Tribune*. "It's a great feeling. Maybe they're starting to accept me as a ballplayer." In his eleventh major-league season, Carew was certainly giving the fans reason to appreciate him. The four hits improved him to 19-for-32 (.594) in his last eight games. Over the previous twenty-two games, Carew was 40-for-82 (.488).

Trying to become the first major-leaguer to hit .400 in a season since Ted Williams in 1941, Carew got three more hits the next night in the Twins' 10–3 victory over Milwaukee, raising his average to .408. Carew finished the season with a .388 batting average to earn his sixth A.L. batting title. Despite falling short of .400, he became the first major-league player to hit over .380 since Williams had batted .388 in 1957.

The Twins, dubbed "the Lumber Company" and leading the major leagues in batting, faded down the stretch in 1977. They won just seven of twenty-five games in September, finishing with an 84–77 record—seventeen and one-half games behind the Kansas City Royals, who won 102 games. The following year, Carew won a seventh A.L. batting title to cap his final season with the Twins.

December 15, 1978
Not Ready for Prime Time

Women's Pro Basketball Emerges Prematurely

In the mid-1970s, the only professional basketball opportunities for women were in Europe. But five years after federal legislation—Title IX—had expanded college athletics for women and two years after women's basketball was introduced as an Olympic sport, the formation of the Women's Professional Basketball League in 1978 generated professional opportunities in the United States. To paraphrase an old adage, however, there is no sadder thing than a great idea whose time has not come. The eight-team league, with franchises in Illinois, Iowa, Minnesota, New Jersey, New York, Ohio, Texas, and Wisconsin was short-lived.

The league held its first player draft in July 1978. The Minnesota franchise, owned by a group of investors led by Gordon Nevers, selected the University of Tennessee's Trish Roberts, member of the 1976 U.S. Olympic Team and captain of the 1977 U.S. National Team. The first game in league history was played December 9 in Milwaukee, where the Milwaukee Does lost to the Chicago Hustle 92–87 before 7,824 fans.

The Minnesota Fillies made their debut six days later at home against the Iowa Cornets. An announced Met Center crowd of 4,102 watched the Cornets beat the Fillies 103–81. The Fillies, playing without Roberts while she recovered from knee surgery, led 18–16 after one quarter, but the Cornets took control with a 13–2 run in the second and opened a 49–36 lead at halftime. Joan Uhl scored 22 points to lead the Cornets, who made 45 of 97 field goal attempts. Brenda Chapman scored 23 points and Donna Wilson collected 20 for the Fillies, who shot just 34 percent (31-of-90) from the field. "I'm not disappointed," Fillies coach Julia Yeater told the *St. Paul Pioneer Press*. "Believe it or not, we're a strong outside shooting team.

But tonight our shots wouldn't fall. We played good ball for 10 minutes. Now all we have to do is play it for 48."

Nevers reported that the team was hoping for a crowd of seven thousand for its first game. Some of the spectators had been given complimentary tickets. "I'm a born optimist," Nevers told the *St. Paul Pioneer Press*. "If I wasn't, I wouldn't have gotten involved in this. We're not expecting everything to go perfect. We know there will be hard times. But we're expecting our attendance to improve and we're expecting our ballclub to improve."

Nevers estimated that the team needed to average thirty-five hundred spectators to break even. "You know everybody wants to know how much money me and my investors are going to lose," Nevers told the *St. Paul Pioneer Press*. "Well let me tell you this: if nobody—not a single fan—comes, we're still going to play our 17 games at home and 17 away. And Gordy Nevers and his investors will laugh all the way to the poor house."

According to the *Pioneer Press*, Fillies forward Lynette Sjoquist told Nevers after the game, "Don't you worry about a thing. We're going to make it . . . just watch."

Despite the loss and the small crowd, Fillies players were ecstatic. "Me, a pro basketball player? I couldn't believe it. I always thought this was a dream that wouldn't happen in my lifetime," Deb Prevost, a guard from Eastern Montana, told the *Minneapolis Tribune*. Prevost, who didn't have a team to play on until she was a senior in high school, added, "For me, the timing is perfect."

Two days later, a crowd of fewer than two thousand showed up to see the Fillies lose to the Houston Angels despite 43 points from Chapman. The Fillies compiled a respectable 17–17 in their first season but finished third in the Midwest Division and missed the WPBL play-offs. Their second season was a success on the court as they went 22–12 and reached the league semifinals. But the third season was a nightmare for the Fillies. Plagued by severe financial problems and low attendance, the team won just seven of thirty-six games.

Other teams faced the same obstacles, and the league folded at the end of the season. While the three-year experiment wasn't a success, it provided women's basketball fans with a glimpse of things to come [see pages 235–36].

Brenda Chapman (15) scored 23 points for the Minnesota Fillies in the state's first regular-season professional women's basketball game.

Miracle on Ice, Part II

U.S. Hockey Team Stuns U.S.S.R.

The challenge facing the U.S. Olympic hockey team on a Friday night in Lake Placid, New York, was so daunting, many observers considered it impossible to overcome. In deference to the task at hand, coach Herb Brooks kept his pregame talk short.

To win the gold, the United States would have to beat the Soviet Union in the first game of the medal round. While the U.S. team was primarily made up of college players, ages nineteen to twenty-five, the veteran Soviet Union team included six members who were playing in their third Olympics. Further, the Russians had not lost in Olympic competition in twelve years, winning all but one of the gold medals in the last twenty-four. In 1979, the Russians had beaten the National Hockey League's all-star team and then, two weeks before traveling to Lake Placid, they had easily defeated the Americans 10–3 in an exhibition at New York City's Madison Square Garden. Brooks, on a leave of absence after coaching the Gophers to the NCAA title the previous year, conceded to the *Minneapolis Tribune*, "we could play our best game and still get blown out."

Brooks's analysis was half-right. He told the *Tribune* that the American team, which included twelve Minnesotans on its twenty-player roster, had been "in awe" of the Russians in the exhibition game two weeks earlier. "I knew we were in trouble that night," Brooks said, "because our players were applauding the great Russian players."

But the Americans, who had won four consecutive games after a tie with Sweden, weren't star-struck on February 24. Although the Russians, having survived upset bids by Finland and Canada in their preceding two games, held one-goal leads on three occasions in the first two periods, the Americans were able to tie the score each time. The Russians

U.S. goalie Jim Craig helped his team to a gold-medal victory over Finland.

U.S. Olympic hockey team members celebrate after their upset victory over the heavily favored Soviet team in 1980.

opened the scoring at 9:12 of the first period, but former Gopher Buzz Schneider tied the score five minutes later. With two and one-half minutes left in the period, the Russians scored to make it 2–1. In the closing seconds, David Christian fired a 90-foot shot that Russian goalie Vladislav Tretiak easily stopped. But Tretiak nonchalantly cleared the puck right in front of the net. Mark Johnson outskated two Russian defenders and managed a quick shot past Tretiak, tying the score with one second remaining.

The Russians outshot the Americans 12–2 in the second period and used an early power-play goal to take a 3–2 lead. Eight minutes into the third period, Johnson made his second goal of the game to tie the score. Less than ninety seconds later, Mike Eruzione scored to put the Americans ahead. Led by goalie Jim Craig, the United States hung on for a miraculous 4–3 victory.

"We played with a style of hockey that American kids don't grow up with," Brooks told the *Minneapolis Tribune*. "Tonight, I turned our players loose. I told them to be creative and to play with poise." When asked what he said to the team before the game, Brooks pulled a sheet of paper out of his pocket, telling the *Tribune* that his entire pregame speech was on it: "I said, 'you were born to be a player, you were meant to be here. This moment is yours, you were meant to be here at this time.'"

The stunning victory didn't guarantee the gold medal for the United States, however. Two days after beating the Russians, the Americans rallied from a 2–1 deficit with three third-period goals to beat Finland 4–2 and claim the second hockey gold in U.S. history [see pages 93–95]. "This team has startled the athletic world," Brooks told the *Minneapolis Tribune*. "Not just the hockey world. Whatever you people write, remember these players are deserving. Any father or mother will know how much I love these guys."

The entire country loved the team and Brooks, who twenty years earlier had been cut from the U.S. squad that won the gold at Squaw Valley, California. "After this, everyone will be gone," Brooks said. "Everybody splits. But as years go by, this'll mean something." Brooks was right: nearly twenty years later, *Sports Illustrated* called the team's accomplishment "the greatest sports moment of the twentieth century."

May 12–21, 1981
Hungry Stars Reach for Cup

Stanley Cup Finals Come to Minnesota

After losing 138 more games than they won between 1974 and 1979, the Minnesota North Stars earned their first National Hockey League play-off victory in seven years, defeating the Toronto Maple Leafs in April 1980. The North Stars went on to sweep the Maple Leafs 3–0 and edge the Montreal Canadiens 4–3 to advance to the semifinal round, where their season ended with a 4–1 series loss to the Philadelphia Flyers.

That taste of postseason success left the North Stars hungry for more, and they opened their fourteenth NHL season by losing just twice in the first fifteen games. But after a mere 14 losses in 51 games, the North Stars lost 14 of their last 29 regular-season games, going 10–14–5 in February, March, and April. Despite the slump, which could be partially attributed to injuries—to which the team lost a league-high 322 man-games—the North Stars finished with a 35–28–17 record and 87 points. The point total was the second-best in franchise history, just one shy of the previous season.

After closing out the regular season with an 8–4 loss in Chicago, the North Stars faced an old nemesis in the first round of the play-offs: the Boston Bruins. Never in franchise history had the North Stars managed a victory at Boston Garden, where they had lost twenty-eight games and tied seven. But on April 8, Steve Payne's hat trick—including the game-winning goal in overtime—lifted the North Stars to a 5–4 victory. This triumph was a positive omen, as the North Stars won the next two games against the Bruins (9–6 and 6–3) and then beat the Buffalo Sabres four games to one for a return trip to the semifinals.

The North Stars and the Calgary Flames split the first two games in Calgary before the North Stars' back-to-back victories at the Met Center gave them a 3–1 lead. The Flames avoided elimination with a 3–1 win in Calgary, but then the North Stars earned their first trip

Goalie Gilles Meloche helped the 1980–81 Minnesota North Stars reach the Stanley Cup finals for the first time in franchise history.

to the Stanley Cup finals with a 5–3 victory. The North Stars' foe in the finals: the defending NHL champion New York Islanders.

The best-of-seven series opened May 12 in Nassau County Coliseum on Long Island with the Islanders winning 6–3. Two nights later, the Islanders took a 2–0 series lead with the same score. The tournament then shifted to Bloomington for the third and fourth games. On May 17, in Minnesota's first Stanley Cup game, a Met Center crowd of 15,784 saw the Islanders move within one game of a sweep with a 7–5 victory. The North Stars went into the fourth game on May 19 knowing that just one team in the history of the NHL finals had rallied from a 3–0 deficit to win the series—Toronto over Detroit in 1942. All they wanted was to avoid a sweep.

The *Minneapolis Tribune* reported that coach Glen Sonmor told the players "they have to beat us once and tonight is not the night." Indeed, the North Stars earned a 4–2 win to send the series back to Long Island. Commenting on the victory, rookie goalie Don Beaupre told the *Minneapolis Tribune*, "Going into the season, we really had high hopes of getting into the finals. I think we were meant to be here, and so to go down in four straight would have been very disappointing."

But any expectations of a second North Stars victory disappeared quickly. On May 21, Butch Goring scored twice to help the Islanders take a 3–0 lead in the game's first ten minutes. The Islanders went on to win 5–1, claiming their second straight title. Sonmor told the

After losing the first three games of the series, the North Stars won game four to avoid a sweep by the New York Islanders in the 1981 Stanley Cup finals. Steve Payne (21) scored the game winner.

Tribune, "I've been proud of my guys all season long, and I'm proud of them tonight. The Islanders are an outstanding team that was not really tested or challenged by anyone in the play-offs. They are equipped to become a dynasty, but this is only the first year they have gone through without any flaws. But anybody who wants to be considered the premier team in this league will have to challenge them."

In the play-offs, the Islanders were led by Bryan Trottier, who scored at least one point in each of their eighteen games. Mike Bossy, who had 35 points, also gave a notable performance, earning 17 goals to burnish his regular-season count of 68. Payne, who tied Bossy for the most play-off goals, told the *Minneapolis Tribune,* "I thought the way we played in the play-offs really saved our season." North Stars' captain Paul Shmyr added, "They have an excellent hockey team, and, as far as I'm concerned, the better team won."

The Islanders showed Shmyr knew what he was talking about by winning two more Stanley Cup championships. The North Stars won a division title the next season but lost in the first round of the play-offs. It would be ten years before the North Stars again enjoyed a season like that of 1981.

Metropolitan Stadium, which opened in 1956, played host to the All-Star Game and the World Series in 1965.

September 30, 1981
An Economic Decision

Minnesota Twins Move Indoors

Minnesota Twins owner Calvin Griffith maintained that the argument over whether baseball should be played indoors or outdoors was moot. "I don't think you'll find anybody around here who will argue with you baseball wasn't meant to be played outdoors in the sunshine," Griffith told the *Minnesota Daily*. "I still believe that. But with the economics of the game of baseball today, I think the majority of owners would prefer to have a stadium that would guarantee that they can get their 80 games in each year. Now we can stop worrying about the weather because when there is a game scheduled, we know we'll get it in."

After debuting in Minnesota in 1961, the Twins played 1,671 games in twenty-one seasons at Metropolitan Stadium. In that span, only eighty-two games, an average of four per season, were rained out. Griffith explained that the rainout statistic was misleading, telling the *Daily*, "In Minnesota, we play so many games, especially in April, May and September that we shouldn't play, but we do because we simply have to get them in. I don't like seeing fans at a game freezing and wet." Beginning in April 1982, when they moved into a domed stadium in downtown Minneapolis, the Twins would no longer have to worry about canceling games for midsummer thunderstorms or early- or late-season snowstorms. But first they had to play one last game in less-than-ideal weather conditions at Met Stadium.

During the Twins' final season at Metropolitan Stadium—interrupted by a fifty-day strike between June 12 and August 1 and punctuated by seven rainouts—there hadn't been many fans. The Twins drew fewer than five hundred thousand that summer, an average of seven thousand per home game. The only American League team still owned by a family instead of a corporation was hoping for one last big gate heading into the off-season. With favorable weather conditions, a crowd of twenty-five to thirty thousand was expected to see

the final baseball game at Met Stadium. But Mother Nature didn't cooperate, producing occasional rain, temperatures in the low fifties, and windy conditions. Despite the weather, this was one of those games that fell into the "had-to-be-played" category. "At the end of a season, you don't make that [revenue] up," Griffith told the *Minnesota Daily*. "With a baseball team all the money is going out in the winter." He estimated that canceling the last game would cost the franchise one hundred thousand dollars.

A crowd of 15,900—the second largest closing-day attendance for the Twins—gathered to pay their respects to the Met. Two banners in left field expressed the fans' sentiments: "Save the Met," and "Farewell old friend." For most of the game, while the Twins were losing to the Kansas City Royals, the fans were subdued. But in the middle of the seventh inning, "Take Me Out to the Ballgame" seemed to be sung with special fervor, and in the bottom of the ninth, after the Twins lost 5–2, the fans gave the stadium a farewell standing ovation.

Coincidentally, the Twins' first game at Met Stadium had been played in similar weather conditions and also resulted in a loss.

When the stadium opened in 1956—the Minneapolis Millers called it home for five seasons—it was pronounced by baseball observers to be "the last word in stadium construction." The cantilever structure meant there weren't any obstructed-view seats. Griffith summarized the stadium's legacy: "it was a hell of a business venture. The people built it with private money. There was no bond issue, no government or city money. They were very happy with it and had a different feeling about the park. It was their park." Over the years, various expansions pushed the final cost of the stadium to $10.4 million.

Griffith, who had moved the franchise to Minnesota in 1961 after sixty years in the nation's capital, told the *Minnesota Daily* he would always think fondly of Met Stadium: "There were a lot of memorable events in this stadium. There were a lot of rock concerts here, but rock concerts are a dime a dozen. The two biggest [events] I remember were the All-Star game played here in 1965 and the World Series the same year. You know you only get to host an All-Star game every 26 years and the World Series was unforgettable. Both were played in good weather."

Griffith wasn't worried that fans wouldn't want to watch the Twins indoors: "You know there are always people who say 'you won't see me going to a game in the dome.' It's like when the Met was built, St. Paul people said they wouldn't go to Bloomington. But you always end up seeing them at games. I think once you get baseball in your blood, you'll go to the games no matter where they're played. And once people get acclimated to the surroundings and parking downtown, they'll come."

The following April 6, the Twins played their first regular-season game in the $55 million Hubert Humphrey Metrodome. Outside the temperature was a frosty twenty-eight degrees. Inside the dome, where it was a balmy seventy, 52,279 fans watched the Seattle Mariners defeat the Twins 11–7.

November 21, 1981
The Brickyard Closes

Gophers Play Final Game
at Memorial Stadium

After years of debate, construction on a domed stadium in downtown Minneapolis finally began in December 1979. The Minnesota Twins and the Minnesota Vikings agreed to leave Bloomington's Metropolitan Stadium to play in the Metrodome, which would be ready in April 1982. The Metropolitan Sports Facilities Commission wanted a third tenant for the stadium—the University of Minnesota football team.

Memorial Stadium, which took just seven months to build, had been home to the Gophers since 1924, and the decision to vacate it wouldn't be quick or easy. In spring 1981, the University of Minnesota and the stadium commission began discussions about the Gophers joining the Vikings and Twins in the dome, but the Gophers went into the 1981 season with those negotiations unresolved. Their schedule included seven games at the 63,000-seat stadium located at the corner of Oak Street Southeast and University Avenue Southeast. The Gophers won their first four home games before losing to number fifteen Michigan in front of a season-high crowd of 52,875.

The following week, the Gophers stunned number eighteen Ohio State 35–31 at Memorial Stadium, their first victory over the Buckeyes since 1949. The Gophers were led by quarterback Mike Hohensee, who completed 37 of 67 passes (both school records) for 444 yards and five touchdowns. The victory improved the Gophers' record to 6–3 and, with two regular-season games remaining, opened the door for a possible bowl-game bid. But the following week, the Gophers lost at Michigan State 43–36.

The Gophers' regular-season finale was at home against rival Wisconsin. Two days after the Twin Cities received twelve inches of snow—the biggest snowfall in four years—a crowd of 47,125, the second largest of the season, showed up to watch the Gophers and Badgers.

Memorial Stadium, at the corner of Oak Street Southeast and University Avenue Southeast, was home to Gopher football for fifty-eight seasons.

Gopher fans had two questions: Would a victory secure a bowl bid? And would the game be the final one played in Memorial Stadium?

Late in the fourth quarter, it looked like the Gophers had a ready answer to the first question. Behind Hohensee, the Gophers rallied from a 17–7 halftime deficit to take a 21–20 lead in the fourth quarter. Hohensee, who was 11-of-18 for 178 yards in the second half, threw a four-yard pass to Chester Cooper for the go-ahead touchdown. But the Badgers rallied behind backup quarterback Randy Wright, who engineered a six-play, 85-yard drive—culminated by a seven-yard touchdown pass with 1:05 remaining—for a 26–21 victory.

The key play of the winning drive occurred with 1:41 on the clock and with the Badgers at their own 32-yard line. Due to miscommunication, the Gophers were left with just ten players on the field. Wright took advantage of the situation to complete a 49-yard pass, which gave the Badgers a first down at the Gophers' 18-yard line. Two plays later, the Badgers, who had needed just forty-nine seconds to cover the eighty-five yards, scored. The victory gave the Badgers a spot in the Garden State Bowl and decisively answered the fans' first question.

As for the second question, one month earlier University of Minnesota president C. Peter Magrath had told the university's board of regents he wasn't prepared to recommend that the Gophers play in the Metrodome. At the October 16 meeting, Magrath explained that the stadium commission had presented a financial package that didn't make sense for the University, charging it one hundred seventy-five thousand dollars to have the football team play in the dome. The following February the board received an update. One of the items under discussion was a questionnaire, distributed to the university's 4,557 dormitory residents, consisting of a single question: "Do you feel that the Gopher football team should be moved to the domed stadium?" Of the 2,116 responses, the result was 3-to-1 in opposition of the move.

The discussion was carried over to the regents' March meeting, at which Magrath reversed his position, recommending that the Gophers move to the dome. Following an extensive discussion, the regents voted 10–1 in favor of the move with the stipulation that the situation be reviewed at the end of each of the next three years. "The contract is a good deal, fair to both sides and has the right sorts of protection for both sides," Magrath told the regents.

In the end, a number of factors led to the agreement. Of critical importance, Magrath told the board, was the fact that Memorial Stadium, which had cost $572,000 to build in 1924, would need extensive and expensive renovation within five to ten years if it were to remain in use for Gopher football. "I don't think that's a good investment for us to be considering in light of other University needs," Magrath said. At the same meeting, the regents had gotten their first look at a proposed budget for the following year, which included $15.4 million in cuts. The regents agreed that Memorial Stadium would be maintained for three years in case the University decided to bring the football team back on campus.

Despite leaving the door open, the Gophers had found a new home. Having averaged 43,000 fans in their final season outdoors, the Gophers averaged nearly 59,000, 49,000, 52,000, and 61,000 per game in their first four seasons in the dome. Memorial Stadium—the beloved Brickyard—was demolished in 1989.

Gopher quarterback Mike Hohensee drops back to pass against Wisconsin in the Gophers' final game at Memorial Stadium.

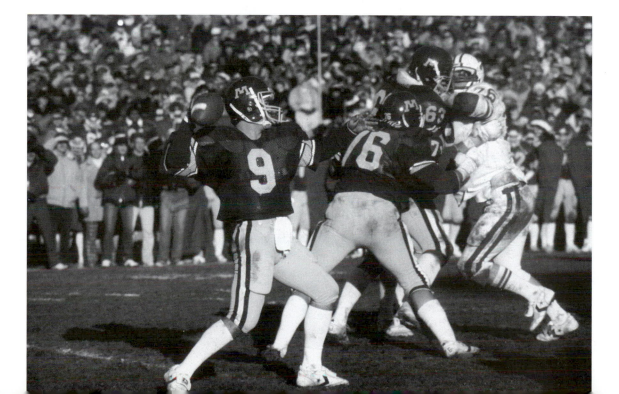

Take-home Memories

Last Game at Met Produces Souvenir Hunters

During the night before the Minnesota Twins' final game in Metropolitan Stadium, someone managed to steal home plate. Later that day, following the Twins' loss to the Kansas City Royals, hundreds of fans gathered on the field, searching for mementos. For the most part, the fans went home empty-handed.

Fans attending the final Minnesota Vikings game at the Met were more determined to claim souvenirs. Determined and, apparently, resourceful. Two days prior to the game, Vikings general manager Mike Lynn issued a statement, reported in the *Minneapolis Tribune:* "We have received information recently that people are planning to take tools to the stadium for the purpose of getting souvenirs, such as seats. We want to remind those people that Metropolitan Stadium is private property and that taking anything from the stadium is illegal." To discourage the souvenir-seekers, the Vikings tripled their security force for the game.

After twenty-one seasons at the Met, the Vikings went into their final home game in a slump—a 7–8 record and a four-game losing streak—and officially eliminated from play-off contention—the previous day's victory by the New York Giants destroying their postseason hopes. Having lost to the Detroit Lions 45–7 in Detroit the previous week, the Vikings hoped to end the season on a positive note. A victory over the Kansas City Chiefs would be the team's 100th at Met Stadium, and late in the game, it looked like the Vikings would reach that milestone.

Trailing by four with 4:30 remaining, the Vikings, who had managed to score only two field goals to that point, drove sixty-six yards for a first down at the Chiefs' 5-yard line. But they failed to score on their first three downs, and then the drive ended with an incomplete pass on fourth down with nineteen seconds remaining. The Chiefs held on for a 10–6 victory.

Receiver Carlos Carson helped the Kansas City Chiefs outlast the Minnesota Vikings and defensive back Willie Teal in the final football game played at Metropolitan Stadium.

In his fifteenth season with the Vikings, coach Bud Grant wasn't sentimental about the final sporting event at Met Stadium, telling the *Minneapolis Tribune:* "People aren't going to remember for very long what happened here today, because there's going to be a new game, a new hero, a new set of circumstances, a new team. In our business, tomorrow morning's newspaper is what you're looking for, not yesterday's. While there are a lot of good memories, there are also some bitter ones like this. You can't go home and look at your wall and think of all the good things that happened. Football is the type of game where you have to forget about the winning as quickly as you forget about the losing. You do the best you can. Then you go home and have supper."

But before many of the 41,110 fans went home, they tried to take a piece of the Met with them. In the game's final minutes, fans started dismantling the seats and bleachers, and when the game ended, thousands stormed the field. The goal posts came down first. Fans scaled the giant scoreboard, stripping away letters, speakers, and light bulbs. In the rest rooms, urinals and plumbing fixtures were taken. Anything that could be removed was.

Ninety minutes after the game ended, with dusk and freezing rain falling, the stadium was cleared.

Minneapolis police officer Sergeant John Brodin — one of about fifty officers working the game — described the postgame bedlam to the *Minneapolis Tribune:* "We knew what was going to happen, you could just feel it. You can understand that kind of behavior at a rock concert, but not at a Vikings' game. I've worked about 100 rock concerts and I've never seen anything like this. We couldn't even consider arrests. Anything short of homicide, there was just no way. We were so short of people compared to the number of fans."

The *Minneapolis Tribune* also reported that before he left the stadium, Vikings tight end Joe Senser walked into the stands for a final look. Asked if he was saying good-bye, he responded, "No, I was seeing how much damage had been done."

The stadium—a mecca for Vikings and Twins fans for twenty-one years, playing host to over seventeen hundred regular-season events—was eventually demolished to make room for a mecca of a different sort: the Mall of America.

Vikings fans were determined to claim a piece of the scoreboard after the final event held at the Met.

A Surprising Decision

Bud Grant Announces Retirement

Bud Grant had enjoyed the limelight for nearly forty years. At the University of Minnesota, he was a two-time all–Big Ten Conference selection in football and a three-year starter in basketball. He played professional basketball with the Minneapolis Lakers and professional football in the National and Canadian Football Leagues before starting his coaching career with the Winnipeg Blue Bombers of the CFL. But it was as coach of the Minnesota Vikings that Grant truly made his mark. In 1968, his second season in Minnesota, he coached the team to its first-ever play-off berth, and between 1968 and 1983 he led the Vikings to eleven division titles, twelve play-off appearances, and four Super Bowls.

The unflappable coach always told his players, "don't make a decision before you have to." Grant heeded his own words. On January 27, 1984, about five weeks after the Vikings had closed out an 8–8 season with a 20–14 victory over the Cincinnati Bengals, Grant announced he was retiring after seventeen seasons as the Vikings' coach. Grant's public announcement came two days after he informed Vikings general manager Mike Lynn of his decision and they flew to Hawaii to tell Vikings president Max Winter in person.

Although the Vikings had lost six of their final eight games and missed the play-offs for the third time in six seasons, Grant's decision was unexpected. The fifty-seven year old had one year remaining on a three-year contract, and in his time with the team he had coached the Vikings to a 151–87–5 record (.629 winning percentage). "In my mind timing is a most important thing," Grant told Sid Hartman of the *Minneapolis Star Tribune*. "I decided this

Bud Grant lettered in baseball, basketball, and football at the University of Minnesota before playing professional basketball with the Minneapolis Lakers.

Bud Grant surprised many when he announced his retirement from coaching at the age of fifty-seven.

was the time to quit. There wasn't any pressure on me. There are lot of things I want to do while I still have my health."

"Bud surprised me when he told me Wednesday of his decision," Lynn told Hartman. "We spent three to four hours discussing the subject. There certainly wasn't any pressure for him to quit. I tried very hard to talk him out of it. I told him we would do anything monetarily or otherwise, if he would stay."

Winter, who had known Grant for more than three decades, was equally surprised: "Bud's decision was a real shock. I've never thought the time would come that he would want to quit coaching. But we will keep him active even though he is out of coaching. I started him as a player with the Lakers 35 years ago. Now it is hard to believe that he doesn't want to coach any more. In my book, he is the best football coach who ever lived."

Vikings players were also stunned by the news. Running back Teddy Brown told the *Star Tribune*, "I don't know if the Vikings will be better and I don't know if the Vikings will be worse, but I do know this: the Vikings will not be the same."

Agreeing to stay on as a consultant to the team, Grant convinced Lynn and Winter to retain all of his coaching staff for at least one season. They named a successor to Grant within seventy-two hours, promoting thirty-eight-year-old assistant Les Steckel to head coach. Under Steckel, the Vikings split their first four 1984 regular-season games but won just one of their last twelve games to finish the season with a 3–13 record. They concluded the season with their sixth consecutive loss, 38–14 to Green Bay on December 16. The next day Steckel was fired, and two days later the Vikings announced Grant would return as coach. Grant coached the Vikings to a 7–9 season in 1985 before stepping down and being replaced by long-time assistant Jerry Burns.

This time the retirement was permanent. Grant left behind a legacy as one of the top coaches in the history of professional football. The first person elected to both the Pro Football Hall of Fame and the Canadian Football Hall of Fame, he had won 290 games in twenty-eight seasons as a head coach and had coached the Vikings to eleven division championships and four Super Bowls.

June 22, 1984
A Sad Day for Calvin

Griffith Sells Twins to Carl Pohlad

During his tenure as the principal owner of the Minnesota Twins, Calvin Griffith enjoyed some tremendous highs and endured some incredible lows. He was hailed as a hero when he relocated the Washington Senators to Minnesota in October 1960 [see pages 103–4]. His team had strong support—leading the American League in attendance for the 1960s—and was cheered greatly when it won the 1965 American League pennant and the 1969 and 1970 A.L. West Division titles. But there were also difficult times, especially after several star players were traded or allowed to leave via free agency because the franchise couldn't afford to keep them. The low point may have been when Griffith made critical remarks about fans and players in a speech given in Waseca, Minnesota, in September 1978.

Two months after the speech, the *Minneapolis Tribune* published the results of its "Minnesota Poll," which showed that 57 percent of

Calvin Griffith's family owned the Washington Senators/Minnesota Twins franchise for seventy-two years.

those surveyed considered Griffith's speech a "major blunder." But in the same poll, 40 percent responded that too much was made of the incident, and 85 percent said they thought the team should stay in Minnesota. Even those who professed no interest in the Twins indicated, by a 2-to-1 margin, that they preferred to see the team remain in the state.

The seventy-two-year-old Griffith had a lifelong relationship with baseball. After starting out as a batboy for the Washington Senators, who were owned by his uncle Clark Griffith, Calvin Griffith would eventually hold three titles with the Twins: chairman of the board, president, and general manager. But in the late 1970s and early 1980s, baseball's changing financial climate made it difficult for the Twins, the only remaining American League team not owned by a corporation, to compete. Eventually, Griffith decided to sell the franchise that had been owned by his family for seventy-two years.

On June 22, 1984, Griffith signed a letter of intent to sell the majority ownership of the Twins to Minneapolis businessman Carl Pohlad for $36 million. Griffith had resisted several offers to buy the team, including some higher bids: "We got two offers for $50 million," Griffith told the *Minneapolis Star Tribune*. "But those involved relocating the team and we didn't want to do that."

Pohlad told Sid Hartman of the *Star Tribune*, "I've been trying to buy the Twins for the past 10 years. I told Calvin many times that when he was ready to sell the club, I'd be interested." The two signed the agreement in an on-field ceremony prior to the Twins–White Sox game. A Metrodome crowd of 21,919 gave Griffith a standing ovation as he left the field. One sign read: "Dear Calvin: Thanks for the memories."

Under the terms of the agreement, Griffith remained with the team as a consultant. He told the *Star Tribune*, "This was the toughest day of my life. I never thought it would happen. I planned to die owning the team. It will be a sad day when it is finally done. The Griffiths have been in baseball since 1891." Griffith admitted that he would miss talking to the press: "I think I've been pretty good copy for a lot of them. I've tried to be honest. Nobody can always be right. I've been criticized a few times. But if you are never crucified and criticized, you haven't done anything."

Instrumental in bringing major league baseball to the Upper Midwest, Griffith had endured good times and bad in Minnesota. He left behind a franchise that would soon reward fans' patience.

October 25, 1987
Shedding a Reputation

Twins Win World Series

Over the years, Minnesota's professional sports teams had developed a "runner-up" reputation. This unwelcome status commenced with the Minnesota Twins in 1965 [see pages 112–15], grew with the Vikings' four Super Bowl losses in seven years, and was further proven with the North Stars' defeat in the 1981 Stanley Cup finals [see pages 175–78]. But Minnesota's reputation was suddenly revised when, on a late October day in 1987, the Minnesota Twins defeated the St. Louis Cardinals 4–2 in game seven of the World Series. To call the Twins' championship—the first for a Minnesota professional sports franchise since the Minneapolis Lakers won the NBA title in 1954—"unexpected" would be a fairly significant understatement.

In 1986, the Twins lost ninety-one games—including a frustrating twenty-seven in which they had been tied or ahead after seven innings. By 1987, they had developed a solid nucleus of players but still had trouble away from home, winning just 29 of 81 regular-season road games. But the Twins made up for their poor showing on the road by compiling a 56–25 record at home.

On September 27, 1987, Bert Blyleven pitched a five-hitter in an 8–1 victory over Kansas City, and, miraculously, the Twins clinched at least a tie for the A.L. West title. The next day, they sealed their first division title in seventeen years by rallying for a 5–3 victory over Texas. Having lost their final five regular-season games to finish with an 85–77 record—the ninth-best in the major leagues—the Twins weren't given much of a chance against the A.L. East champion Detroit Tigers, who had ninety-eight regular-season wins. Additionally, the Twins had lost three straight to the Tigers at midseason by a combined score of 26–3. But the Twins defeated the Tigers 8–5 in game one of the American League Championship Series—their first postseason victory in twenty-two years. They went on to win the series, four games to one, advancing to the World Series against the National League champion St. Louis Cardinals.

The World Series opened with the Twins winning the first two games at home by scores of 10–1 and 8–4. Play then shifted to St. Louis, where the Cardinals won the next three games, 3–1, 7–2, and 4–2, to move within one victory of winning the best-of-seven series. After a day off, the series returned to the Metrodome. Four and one-half innings into game six, the Cardinals had a 5–2 lead, but, sparked by Kent Hrbek's grand slam and four hits from Kirby Puckett, the Twins rallied for an 11–5 victory to force game seven.

In the final game, the Cardinals again took an early lead, the score 2–1 in the fourth. But the Twins, who had four players hit at least twenty-eight home runs during the regular season, tied the game on a single by Puckett and scored the go-ahead run after three walks and an infield single by Greg Gagne. The Twins added a run in the eighth inning to take a two-run lead. Frank Viola, who had retired 18 of 20 hitters after pitching out of a second-inning jam, gave way in the ninth to reliever Jeff Reardon, who pitched a perfect inning to save the victory.

At 10:29 P.M. on October 25, Twins fans were finally able to chant "We're Number One." Spectators were so mesmerized that many of the more than fifty-five thousand in attendance remained in the Metrodome long after the final out, waiting patiently for team members to return to the field for curtain calls. Thousands of jubilant fans jammed the streets of downtown Minneapolis, some of them climbing light posts and traffic lights.

The 1987 World Series was notable for two reasons: first, the home team had won all seven games for the first time in eighty-four World Series, and, second, the Twins' 85–77 regular-season record was the worst of any World Series champion. Baseball commissioner Peter Ueberroth summarized the euphoria for Sid Hartman of the *Star Tribune:* "Three years ago when I became commissioner, I was

Kirby Puckett's defense helped the Minnesota Twins win their first World Series in 1987.

Frank Viola was 3–1 in the Twins' 1987 postseason and the winning pitcher in game seven of the World Series.

told that this area shouldn't have a baseball franchise. But these fans proved everybody wrong and this has developed into one of the best franchises in baseball. . . . These are the best baseball fans I have ever seen. . . . These are not only great fans but polite fans."

Those fans wouldn't have to wait too long to be rewarded again [see pages 203–6].

The Twins and the St. Louis Cardinals met for the first-ever indoor World Series game on October 17, 1987.

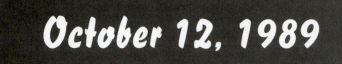

A Blockbuster Deal

Vikings Acquire Herschel Walker

The day after the Minnesota Vikings concluded the 1984 season with a 3–13 record—considered by many to be the franchise's lowest point—team general manager Mike Lynn did two things. First, he fired coach Les Steckel. Then, he met with the players and promised to upgrade the team's talent, embarking on a five-year rebuilding plan that would restore their Super Bowl contention capabilities.

In the third year of Lynn's plan, the Vikings made the play-offs as a wild-card team—their first play-off appearance in five seasons—and reached the National Football Conference championship game, losing to the Washington Redskins 17–10. The following season, 1988, the Vikings compiled the most victories since 1976, going 11–5 and reaching the second round of the play-offs. Lynn had succeeded in upgrading the team's talent in a short time: following the dismal 1984 season, the Vikings had just one Pro Bowl player—kicker Jan Stenerud—but after the 1988 season, the Vikings sent eight players to the Pro Bowl.

Lynn added two more all-stars in 1989. On draft day, he acquired linebacker Mike Merriweather from the Pittsburgh Steelers. But it was Lynn's second trade that year that the *Minneapolis Star Tribune* deemed "the most-covered—if not the biggest story—in Minnesota sports history."

After going 1–2 in their first three games, the Vikings beat Tampa Bay and Detroit to improve to 3–2. Around that time, rumors began circulating that the winless Dallas Cowboys were considering trading star running back Herschel Walker. The Cleveland Browns, hoping to contend for the American Football Conference title, were interested in acquiring Walker. So was Lynn, who thought Walker, a former University of Georgia and U.S. Football

Herschel Walker was the Vikings' leading rusher from 1989 to 1991.

In 1989, the Vikings acquired Herschel Walker from the Dallas Cowboys in exchange for five players and eight draft choices.

League standout who had rushed for more than fifteen hundred yards for the Cowboys the previous season, could make the Vikings a championship-caliber team.

After several days of negotiations, on October 12 Lynn and the Cowboys agreed on a blockbuster deal. The Vikings sent five players (Issiac Holt, David Howard, Darrin Nelson, Jesse Solomon, and Alex Stewart) and eight draft picks to Dallas for the twenty-seven-year-old running back. The trade dwarfed an earlier one long considered to be the biggest in team history—when the Vikings re-acquired quarterback Fran Tarkenton in 1972. Vikings coach Jerry Burns tried to be diplomatic regarding Walker. "He's not responsible for getting us to the Super Bowl," Burns told the *Minneapolis Star Tribune*. "He's just another cog in that direction."

At his introductory news conference, Walker was tactful, telling the *Star Tribune*, "I don't know whether I'm the answer or not. Minnesota is a great place to play football and a great place to live. That's the key here, I'm going to be thrilled to be here."

Walker was the Vikings' first all-pro at the running back position since Chuck Foreman in 1975–76. "I hope Walker can do for us what Foreman did," Burns told the *Star Tribune*. "Walker is a great player. Like Foreman he is a great receiver coming out of the backfield. He is an excellent runner like Chuck was."

The previous season, Walker had caught 53 passes for 505 yards to go more than 2,000 yards in total offense. In his first three seasons with the Cowboys, he had rushed for 3,142 yards and caught 189 passes for 2,057 yards. Once onboard, Walker paid immediate dividends for the Vikings. Three days after the trade, on his first play from scrimmage against the Green Bay Packers, he gained forty-seven yards. With just two days of practice to learn the Vikings' system, Walker rushed for 148 yards in eighteen carries. He also caught one pass for seven yards and returned two kickoffs for forty yards as the record Metrodome crowd of 62,075 roared its approval. The first Viking to rush for more than one hundred yards in thirty games, Walker helped the Vikings end a four-game losing streak against the Packers, 26–14, and move into a tie for first place in the NFC Central.

"One thing I can do is learn a system," Walker told the *Star Tribune*. "I've learned systems overnight. When I went to Dallas, I learned it within a week. When I go into a game, I want to be prepared because that's when I feel at home."

The Vikings won four of their first five games with Walker in the lineup before suffering back-to-back one-point losses on the road, to Philadelphia and Green Bay (in Milwaukee). But they regrouped and won three of their final four regular-season games to claim their first NFC Central title since 1980. The season ended abruptly with a first-round play-off loss to the 49ers in San Francisco, leaving Minnesotans to wonder if Lynn's rebuilding efforts would have the intended results. They would find out in the next two seasons.

The NBA Returns

Timberwolves Take the Floor

Although the Twin Cities had been instrumental to the initial success of the fledgling National Basketball Association in the 1950s, Minnesota was left without a team in 1960, when the Minneapolis Lakers relocated to Los Angeles [see pages 99–102]. For the next twenty-five years, the only professional basketball in the Twin Cities was a two-year fling with the American Basketball Association in the late 1960s. Not surprisingly, when the NBA announced in the mid-1980s that it wanted to expand, Minnesotans jumped at the chance to lure the NBA back to the state.

Governor Rudy Perpich and two businessmen interested in owning an NBA team, Marv Wolfenson and Harvey Ratner, agreed there was one man who could lend credibility to their quest. They asked former Minneapolis Lakers center George Mikan, the league's first superstar, to join their effort to land an expansion team. Mikan and other interested parties worked for more than a year on the presentation they made to the league's expansion committee on April 3, 1987. Pending the approval of the league's board of directors, the committee agreed that Minnesota should be awarded a franchise.

Nineteen days later, the NBA board of governors voted unanimously to expand by four teams: Miami and Charlotte in 1988–89 and Minnesota and Orlando in 1989–90. The admission fee for each franchise was $32.5 million. The announcement gave Wolfenson and Ratner two and one-half years to build a franchise, and they set to work immediately.

In July 1988, the site for a new arena in downtown Minneapolis was dedicated; during its construction, the team would play in the Metrodome. The next month the franchise named its first coach—former University of Minnesota basketball coach Bill Musselman—

On November 8, 1989, the NBA officially returned to Minneapolis as the Minnesota Timberwolves played host to the Chicago Bulls at the Metrodome.

Tony Campbell led the Timberwolves in scoring in each of their first three seasons.

and on September 17, the franchise unveiled its logo. The nickname had been selected earlier, based on a statewide poll of 842 city councils in which "Timberwolves" was favored by a 2-to-1 margin over "Polars." On June 15, 1989, the Timberwolves took part in the expansion draft, selecting eleven players. (Their first pick was Detroit's Rick Mahorn, who was traded before he could play for the team.)

The Timberwolves opened their first training camp on October 6, 1989. Less than two weeks later, they played their first exhibition game, and on October 18 they opened their six-game preseason schedule against the Los Angeles Lakers at the Metrodome. Before a crowd of 35,156—a record for an NBA exhibition—the Lakers won 100–90. On November 3, just a month after opening camp, the Timberwolves played their inaugural regular-season game, losing to the Seattle SuperSonics, 106–94, in Seattle. They also lost their second game, 93–83, in Portland.

On November 8, the NBA officially returned to Minneapolis after a 29-year absence. A league-record opening-night crowd of 35,427 showed up at the Metrodome to see the Timberwolves take on Michael Jordan and the Chicago Bulls. As they had in their first two regular-season games, the Timberwolves claimed the lead in the fourth quarter but were unable to hang on for the victory. With the Bulls ahead 73–64, the Timberwolves made a 14–4 run to pull ahead 78–77 with 5:19 remaining. A three-pointer by Jordan one minute later gave the Bulls the lead for good as they scored 19 of the game's final 25 points to pull out a 96–84 victory.

"We kept trying to put them out of the game," Jordan told the *Associated Press*, "but they played a good game. It took a lot for us to beat them." Actually, it took 45 points from Jordan for the Bulls to outlast the Timberwolves. Tony Campbell led the Timberwolves in scoring, with 31 points.

Two days later, the Timberwolves earned their first victory, 125–118 over Philadelphia in overtime before 29,117 at the Metrodome. They went on to compile a 22–60 record in their first season while setting an NBA single-season attendance record, drawing 1,072,572 fans. Minnesotans were obviously excited about the NBA's return to the Twin Cities.

October 27, 1991
Worst to First

Puckett, Morris Spur
Twins to the Top

Many observers considered the Minnesota Twins' 1987 World Series title to be a fluke [see pages 193–95]. On paper, maybe it was. That year, the Twins were tenth in the American League in hitting and pitching and just 29–52 on the road. But the Twins surprised many by winning the A.L. West with an 85–77 record and then by beating the Detroit Tigers, who had won ninety-eight games during the regular season, in the A.L. Championship Series. The Twins went on to defeat the St. Louis Cardinals in the World Series.

The Twins actually had a better record the next season, when they won ninety-one games, but they finished second, thirteen games behind A.L. West champion Oakland. Oakland won the A.L. West again in 1989 and in 1990 as the Twins slipped to fifth with eighty wins and eighty-two losses in 1989 and seventh in 1990 with a 74–88 record. The last-place finish in 1990 didn't leave much room for optimism about the Twins' chances in 1991, and that year's slow start didn't help. The Twins were two games under .500 on June 1 after going 9–11 in April and 14–14 in May.

But the Twins quickly turned their season around. On June 1, they defeated Kansas City, the first victory in what would be a club-record 15-game winning streak. Between June 1 and June 16, the Twins defeated Kansas City twice, Baltimore and the New York Yankees three times each, and Cleveland seven times. In all, the Twins compiled a 22–6 record in June— one victory shy of the team's record for most victories in one month, set in July 1969, when the Twins were 23–7 en route to the A.L. West title.

They followed up June with two successful months—going 16–10 in July and 17–12 in August—to fashion a 78–53 record on September 1. Despite a 2–1 loss in Toronto, the Twins

St. Paul native Jack Morris started three games for the Twins in the 1991 World Series and pitched a ten-inning shutout in game seven.

clinched their second A.L. West title in five seasons on September 29, when the second-place Chicago White Sox lost in Seattle. They finished the regular season 95–67—the fourth-best record since the team had moved to Minnesota in 1961—and eight games over the White Sox.

In the A.L. Championship Series, the Twins faced the A.L. East champion Toronto Blue Jays, who had won the regular-season series between the teams 8–4. After splitting the first two play-off games, the Twins won the next three to emerge victorious from the series and complete their worst-to-first transformation.

In the National League, a similar story developed. The Atlanta Braves, who had finished last in the N.L. West in 1990 with a 65–97 record, won the division title with a 94–68 record and then defeated the Pittsburgh Pirates, four games to three, to win the National League title.

The 1991 World Series mirrored the 1987 series, with the home team winning every game—the first two in Minneapolis and the next three in Atlanta. The Braves' victories in games three and four were by one run, but Atlanta pounded out seventeen hits to win game

Bloomington native Kent Hrbek accumulated 20 home runs and 89 RBIs for the Twins during the 1991 regular season.

five 14–5. Back at the Metrodome and needing to win game six to stay alive, the Twins scored twice in the bottom of the first inning for an early 2–0 lead. Atlanta tied it in the top of the fifth, but the Twins regained the lead with a run in the bottom of the fifth. After Atlanta tied again in the seventh, the teams remained deadlocked until the bottom of the eleventh inning, when Kirby Puckett ended the tension with a dramatic home run off Charlie Liebrandt.

The next night—Sunday—would provide even more drama. The Twins rested their hopes on pitcher Jack Morris, who was 18–12 with a 3.43 ERA and ten complete regular-season games. Making his third start in nine days, Morris hooked up with Atlanta's John Smoltz for a pitchers' duel. The two right-handers matched shutout innings through seven, but Atlanta manager Bobby Cox called on his bullpen in the eighth inning, as Mike Stanton pitched the eighth and Alejandro Pena the ninth. Morris meanwhile continued to shut down Atlanta through nine innings, surviving a scare in the eighth when the Braves had runners at second and third with no outs.

Atlanta catcher Greg Olson walks off the field as the Twins celebrate a 1–0 victory in game seven of the 1991 World Series.

When the Twins failed to score in the bottom of the ninth, sending the game into extra innings, Twins manager Tom Kelly wanted to go to his bullpen. But Morris, who had allowed only nine base runners, convinced Kelly to let him pitch the tenth inning, which he escaped unscathed. The Twins rewarded him and their fans when Dan Gladden started off the bottom of the tenth with his third hit of the game. Gladden eventually scored the game's only run when pinch hitter Gene Larkin lofted a fly ball to left center for a game-winning single.

It was only the second time in World Series history that game seven had been decided by a 1–0 score—the first was 1962 when the New York Yankees defeated San Francisco. It was also the first game seven to go into extra innings since 1924.

The Twins and Braves were evenly matched: five of the seven games were decided by one run and four of the games were decided in a team's final at bat. "It was probably the greatest World Series ever," baseball commissioner Fay Vincent told the *Minneapolis Star Tribune.* "I was proud to be here."

For the second time in five seasons, the Twins had astounded their fans and baseball observers with a World Series title.

January 10, 1992
A New Sheriff in Town

Vikings Hire Dennis Green

In 1989, Minnesota Vikings general manager Mike Lynn gambled in the trade for Herschel Walker [see pages 196–99]. Sending Dallas five players and eight draft choices, Lynn bet heavily that the talented running back was the final piece in the puzzle as the Vikings sought to develop a Super Bowl–caliber team. Indeed, after acquiring Walker, the Vikings went on to win the National Football Conference Central—their first division title in nine years. But their season ended with a first-round play-off loss to the San Francisco 49ers.

The Vikings took a giant step backwards in 1990, winning just one of their first seven games. They recovered to win five consecutive match-ups, evening their record at 6–6, but lost their final four regular-season games to miss the play-offs for the first time in four years. In 1991, with Roger Headrick in charge of the team's day-to-day operations, the Vikings again got off to a slow start, winning just three of their first eight games. Despite a strong second half, during which they went 5–3, they missed the play-offs for the second consecutive season. With three games remaining, Jerry Burns announced he would retire at the end of the season. Burns had coached the Vikings to a 52–43 record in his six seasons, but in the final two they were just 14–18.

To find a successor for Burns, Headrick went outside the organization—something the Vikings hadn't done since Bud Grant was hired in 1967. On January 10, 1992, Headrick introduced Dennis Green as the sixth coach in team history. The forty-two-year-old Green had spent the previous three seasons as the head coach at Stanford University, and, prior to that, he had been a member of the San Francisco 49ers' staff for three seasons and the head coach at Northwestern University for five. Headrick cited Green's head coaching experience as one reason for selecting him over New York Jets defensive coordinator Pete Carroll, who had been a Vikings assistant coach from 1985 to 1989. Headrick told the *Minneapolis Star*

Tribune Green was also chosen because of his "forceful personality" and because Headrick valued the viewpoint of a coach who had not previously been affiliated with the team: "He can come in here with the ability not to be bound by the past. This team needed change. It needed something to give it an impetus to turn things around. He is the guy. He's a winner."

Dennis Green, who spent three seasons as the head coach at Stanford, became the Vikings' sixth coach in 1992.

Just the second African American head coach in the National Football League's modern era, following Art Shell of the Los Angeles Raiders, Green promised things would be different: "There's a new sheriff in town. I know we have some tremendous talent. This franchise had some great years in the 1980s, and we look forward to some championship teams in the 1990s. The thing I want to do is bring some strong leadership to this team."

Green's task was challenging in the short term because of the team's age and their lack of high draft picks as a result of the Walker trade. "I don't believe in change for change's sake," Green told the *Star Tribune*. "Let's keep in mind that this is not a team that was 2–14 last year. This was a team that was 8–8 and has a lot of Pro Bowl players."

Green, who had agreed to a four-year contract (with a one-year extension) that the *Star Tribune* reported would pay five hundred fifty thousand dollars in the fourth year, was correct in his assessment. In their first season under Green, the Vikings won seven of their first nine regular-season games en route to an 11–5 record and the NFC Central division title. A first-round play-off loss didn't diminish the quick reversal of fortunes for the franchise. Green's leadership restored the Vikings to the upper echelons of the league as they reached the play-offs in seven of his first eight seasons as coach.

April 13, 1993
Stars Go South

Minnesota Loses NHL Team

Signs that the North Stars' stay in Minnesota was in jeopardy first surfaced during the 1988–89 season, when the team averaged an eleven-year low of 9,795 fans per home game. Then, a year later, the National Hockey League blocked attempts by the North Stars' owners to move the franchise before it was sold for $42 million to Canadian real-estate developer Norm Green, who had been a partner in the Calgary Flames. The North Stars opened the 1990–91 season before a crowd of 5,730 at the Met Center, and they went on to average just 7,838 fans per game, the lowest attendance in the franchise's twenty-four years.

But the North Stars, who finished fourth in the Norris Division, regained their fans' attention in the 1990–91 play-offs. After a six-year play-off drought, they advanced to the finals for just the second time in franchise history. In their first Stanley Cup appearance since 1981 [see pages 175–78], the North Stars lost to the Pittsburgh Penguins, four games to two, but their play-off run had brought fans back to the Met Center—an average of 14,918 spectators for the eleven home play-off games.

The 1991–92 season was a turning point. The team again finished fourth in the Norris Division with a 32–42–6 record, but this time there was no play-off run. In the first round of the play-offs, the North Stars took a 3–1 lead against the Detroit Red Wings, but the Red Wings shut them out in games five and six, 3–0 and 1–0 in overtime, respectively, and went on to win game seven 5–2.

In October 1992, the team signed twenty-two-year-old center Mike Modano to a four-year, $6.75 million contract—the fifth-richest agreement in league history. The North Stars' first-round selection in the 1988 draft, Modano was making six hundred thousand dollars in the final year of his previous contract, and he had scored 29, 28, and 33 goals, respectively, in his first three seasons with the team. Shortly after Modano signed the deal, Green began

North Stars announcer Al Shaver applauds Neal Broten, who holds aloft a gold stick he received as the team's all-time points and assists leader. Shaver was also recognized at this ceremony, on April 10, 1993, for his induction into the NHL Hockey Hall of Fame.

emphasizing his team's dire financial problems. Although Green had set a goal of ten thousand season tickets when he bought the team, there were only fifty-three hundred season-ticket holders for the 1992–93 season. Green suggested remodeling Bloomington's Met Center and connecting it by skyway to its neighbor, the Mall of America. When his proposal fell on deaf ears, Green hinted that the team would be forced to move unless it got an improved lease. Among the new homes mentioned for the North Stars were Minneapolis, St. Paul, and Anaheim, California.

On January 30, 1993, Green received bids from the Minneapolis Target Center and the St. Paul Civic Center and told the *Minneapolis Star Tribune* that he was "not going to lose any more money operating a hockey team." The next month, Green received an offer from businessman Harvey Mackay, who personally guaranteed one thousand season tickets if the team would move to the Target Center. Green rejected the offer.

On March 10, Green announced that he had reached an agreement to move the franchise to Dallas, signing a ten-year lease for the team to play in Reunion Arena, also home to the National Basketball Association's Dallas Mavericks. Green claimed it was strictly a business decision. He told the *Star Tribune* the team had lost $10 million in 1991–92 and would lose another $5 million in 1992–93, despite averaging 13,910 fans per game. Green also confirmed that the day before he reached the agreement with Dallas he had been offered $55 million for the team by a Minneapolis interest. Green said the offer was "inadequate" and he wasn't interested in selling. "This is a sad day for the fans in Minnesota," Green told the *Star Tribune*. "I know that. The finances just didn't work there, for whatever reason."

In their final month in Minnesota, the North Stars battled for a play-off spot. They went into their last home game—April 13 against the Chicago Blackhawks—one point behind the St. Louis Blues for the final Norris Division play-off spot. A crowd of 15,445—the season's largest and its tenth sellout—saw the Blackhawks hang on for a 3–2 victory, their sixth consecutive win over the North Stars. The North Stars closed out the season with two road games and missed the play-offs by one point. Ironically, their 36–36–10 record and 82 points were their best marks in ten seasons. But these numbers and increased fan interest were not enough to keep the team in Minnesota.

Dino Ciccarelli played with the North Stars for nine years and was one of their top scorers, making 55 goals in 1982 and 52 in 1987.

Harris Survives U.S. Amateur

Former Gopher Is Second Minnesotan to Take Title

After excelling in both hockey and golf while at the University of Minnesota, John Harris decided to play professional golf. The second-leading scorer on the Gophers' NCAA hockey championship team and a Big Ten individual golf championship winner—both in 1974—Harris played in mini-tours and some events in Asia before attending the PGA Tour qualifying school. But in January 1979, Harris, who held a degree in business administration, returned to Minnesota and went into the insurance business. "I thought competitive golf was behind me," Harris recalled for the *Minneapolis Star Tribune* years later. "I felt at the time, that I would never play in a tournament again."

Despite this belief, Harris applied to regain his amateur status, a process requiring three years. In 1983, shortly after being redefined as an amateur and while on a family vacation in the Detroit Lakes area, Harris decided to enter the state amateur golf tournament being held nearby. He finished second—by two strokes—behind winner Chris Perry. Harris returned to tournament golf and was five times named the Minnesota Golf Association player of the year. He also gained exposure on a national level as a member of the U.S. team in the Walker Cup, a biennial competition between the United States and Great Britain. In mid-August 1993 at Interlachen, Harris won the match that clinched a U.S. victory. Less than two weeks later, Harris was in the spotlight again when he traveled to Houston, Texas, to compete in the ninety-third annual U.S. Amateur Championship.

In the previous U.S. Amateurs only one Minnesotan—Harrison "Jimmy" Johnston, a St. Paul investment broker—had won the tournament, in 1929 at Pebble Beach, California. Harris became the second to win the U.S. Amateur, but it wasn't easy.

The tournament's format was two rounds of stroke play—to cut the field of 315 players to

Roseau native John Harris claimed the U.S. Amateur trophy in 1993.

John Harris watches a putt on his way to a ten-stroke victory in the 1990 MGA Mid-Amateur Championship.

64—followed by match play. Two years earlier, at Chattanooga, Tennessee, Harris was the co-medalist after stroke play only to lose to Jay Sigel in the first round. But this time was different. On the tournament's first day— a hot and humid August 24—Harris shot a 69 and was just two strokes behind leader Raymond Russell of Scotland. The next day, Harris shot a 73 for a 36-hole total of 142—good enough to tie for fourth place. Among the seven others tied with Harris was a seventeen year old from California named Tiger Woods. Tim Herron, another Minnesotan, was tied for fifth place with a 143.

Harris and Herron were among the thirty-two winners on the first day of match play. Harris defeated John Lindholm of Flint, Michigan, 4-and-2. The second and third rounds of match play were scheduled for August 27, but only the second round was completed after a lightning delay of more than five hours. Harris defeated Danny Green of Jackson, Tennessee, 1-up in nineteen holes to advance. Herron lost by the same score, leaving Harris as the only Minnesotan left in the field.

The next day Harris won two matches—both over Walker Cup teammates—to advance to the semifinals, defeating David Berganio Jr. 3-and-2 in the third round before beating defending champion Justin Leonard 2-and-1 in the quarterfinals. Leonard led Harris 1-up after nine holes, but Harris won the fourteenth with a par before taking the lead for good with a birdie on fifteen. Harris advanced to the 36-hole championship match with a 1-up victory over Bobby Cochran of Cordova, California. Cochran had won the third hole to take the lead—leaving Harris trailing for the fifth consecutive match—but Harris evened the score at number seven before moving ahead at number nine.

The championship match featured Harris and Danny Ellis of Haines City, Florida. The two teed off at 8:45 A.M. on August 30 for the first eighteen holes, then again at 1 P.M. for the final eighteen. After eleven, Harris was 3-up, but Ellis was able to tie the match after eighteen. In the afternoon round, Harris sank a 25-foot birdie putt on number eleven to go 3-up. Ellis bogeyed number fourteen to fall four behind, and on number fifteen—the thirty-third hole of the day—Ellis had another bogey and then conceded a three-foot putt for par to Harris, which gave Harris a 5-and-3 victory.

Harris had survived the week, but he admitted to the *Minneapolis Star Tribune*, "I could have lost . . . early." In his second-round match, Harris was 1-down to Green on the eighteenth hole. "Green was already in with his par," Harris told the *Star Tribune*. "I had a 20-foot putt for a birdie. If I had missed, I would have been on a flight back to the Twin Cities [that] afternoon." Harris sank the putt to even the match and then beat Green with another birdie on the first extra hole.

Then, against Ellis, he saw his early lead dissolve. "I let it get away from me in the morning," Harris told the *Star Tribune*. "I had a virus in my game. I was a little confused to say the least." His caddy—fifteen-year-old son Chris—helped clear his mind. During the break after the first eighteen holes, Harris went to the putting green and practice range, where Chris queried his father: "Chris asked me 'you weren't playing well a month ago . . . what did you do to come out of it?' I said 'I used a forward press,' to get my hands out in front. And Chris said 'Well, you aren't doing that now.' I worked on getting my hands where I wanted them and then went out and played very well in the afternoon round."

The victory earned Harris exemptions to the 1994 Masters and British Open, plus the U.S. Open and five other PGA Tour events. Minnesota's most well-known amateur golfer would eventually give professional golf a second chance when he joined the Senior PGA tour after turning fifty.

February 24–25, 1995

Skating into History

Nation's First Girls' State Hockey Tournament

Women's hockey officially became part of the Minnesota sports landscape in 1986 when the Minnesota Women's Hockey Association was formed, and from that point interest in the sport grew steadily. By 1992, there were thirty-nine girls' and women's teams registered with the Minnesota Amateur Hockey Association, and twenty-five teams in five divisions competed in the MAHA state tournament that year. By fall 1993, eight high schools were fielding girls' hockey teams. Those teams played in relative obscurity before concluding the season in February 1994 with an invitational tournament at Blake, where Blaine/Coon Rapids defeated Anoka/Champlin Park in the tournament final.

"All eight teams were in it, and all of us considered it a real state tournament," Blaine/Coon Rapids coach Marci Bydlon told the *Minneapolis Star Tribune*. "We won the final 3–0, and Laura Tryba scored a hat trick for us in that game." The victory capped an undefeated season for Blaine/Coon Rapids (16–0), during which Tryba, a freshman, had 70 points.

Several weeks after the conclusion of that first season, the Minnesota State High School League representative assembly voted to sanction girls' hockey as a varsity sport, making Minnesota the first state to do so. (In ten states, girls were playing on boys' hockey teams.) At the same meeting, the assembly declined to add "ringette" as a varsity sport for girls. Six teams had played ringette, using a straight stick and a ring instead of a curved stick and a puck, during the just-completed season.

The first "sanctioned" girls' hockey season began in November 1994 with twenty-four varsity and twelve junior varsity teams taking the ice. The first game of the season was between South St. Paul and Holy Angels on November 19. Eighth-grader Kelly Kegley had three goals—including the first ever in state-sanctioned girls' hockey—and two assists to lead South St. Paul to an 8–0 victory over Holy Angels.

Sibley goaltender Mary Jean Schmidt makes a save against South St. Paul, but the Packers' goalie recorded a shutout to send South St. Paul to the championship game of the nation's first girls' state hockey tournament.

The season culminated with four six-team sectional tournaments to determine who would compete in the first girls' state hockey tournament in the nation's history. Apple Valley, Henry Sibley, South St. Paul, and Stillwater won section titles to earn a trip to Aldrich Arena in Maplewood. Those teams, with a combined record of 83–6–4, were greeted by crews from ESPN, CBS, and other national media outlets.

Apple Valley's Tina Olstad, left, Beth Clausen, right, and an unidentified teammate celebrate after their team scored a goal against Stillwater. Apple Valley won the game as well as the championship match against South St. Paul.

Around 1 P.M. on February 24, the historic first puck was dropped for the semifinal between Apple Valley and Stillwater. Apple Valley (22–0–1) was led by Jamie DiGriselles, the *Minneapolis Star Tribune*'s metro player of the year, and freshman Michelle Sikich. DiGriselles paced the Eagles with 78 points (43 goals and 35 assists), while Sikich had 70 points. Sikich scored three goals to lead the Eagles to a come-from-behind 6–4 victory over Stillwater. South St. Paul defeated Henry Sibley 4–0 in the other semifinal.

On Saturday, February 25, a crowd of 3,255 showed up to see who would earn the first state title. The teams were evenly matched: three weeks earlier, Apple Valley and South St. Paul had skated to a 2–2 tie—the only blemish on Apple Valley's record. Sikich scored in the first period and sophomore Betsy Kukowski scored in the third while freshman goalie Jenny Jannett stopped all eighteen shots she faced to lead the Eagles to a 2–0 victory. "This is what we hoped for, but we really didn't expect it," John Bartz of the MSHSL told the *Minneapolis Star Tribune*. "In the 10 years I've been [directing tournaments for the league], this has been the most fun. It's a brand new sport and to see these kids have an opportunity to participate is very gratifying."

The sport quickly grew in popularity. Within eight years, 120 Minnesota teams played varsity girls' hockey, their seasons culminating in a two-class state tournament.

June 28, 1995

New Kid in Town

Timberwolves Draft High School Phenom

The summer of 1995 was a season of changes for the beleaguered Minnesota Timberwolves franchise. Glen Taylor, who purchased the team from Marv Wolfenson and Harvey Ratner, officially took control on March 23. His first major decision—on May 11—was to promote Kevin McHale to executive vice president for basketball operations and to name Flip Saunders general manager. McHale and Saunders immediately began preparing for the National Basketball Association's annual player draft, at which the Timberwolves, who had averaged sixty-one losses per season in their first six years with the league, would have the fifth selection.

McHale and Saunders, who had been teammates at the University of Minnesota, studied the projected top five choices—Maryland forward Joe Smith, North Carolina guard Jerry Stackhouse, Alabama forward Antonio McDyess, North Carolina forward Rasheed Wallace, and Chicago high school star Kevin Garnett. McHale, who reportedly preferred Garnett, told the *Minneapolis Star Tribune* that the "Wolves must do what's best as much for 1999 as 1995."

On the evening of June 28, at Toronto's Skydome, the Golden State Warriors opened the draft by selecting Smith. The next three picks were McDyess, by the Los Angeles Clippers; Stackhouse, by Philadelphia; and Wallace, by Washington. With these choices made, the Timberwolves were free to select the nineteen-year-old Garnett. The *Star Tribune* reported its opinion: "the risks of drafting Garnett are obvious. He could be the next player who, in time, will revolutionize the game with skills previously unseen in such a tall player. Or he could become the next in a long line of NBA casualties destroyed by too much fame, too much money and too much free time at such a young age."

Kevin Garnett is greeted by NBA commissioner David Stern after being selected by the Minnesota Timberwolves in the first round of the 1995 draft.

Kevin Garnett moved into the Timberwolves' starting lineup midway through his rookie season.

The consensus among NBA observers was that the six-foot-eleven Garnett—the first player in twenty years to go directly from high school to the NBA—would have been the number-one draft choice after two years of college. As a high school junior, Garnett had been named Mr. Basketball for South Carolina, and, after moving to Chicago for his senior year, he became Illinois's Mr. Basketball in 1995.

In response to the question, "Is he a franchise player?" Timberwolves coach Bill Blair told the *Star Tribune,* "I can't say that. But this kid does some things that excite you. From a maturity level? No way he can be. He's not ready for the airplanes, the four games in six days, for the free time he's now possessing. Those things we have to help him with. You just hope he's so interested in basketball; you hope he wants to be the best player in the league."

The Timberwolves set up a framework that would protect Garnett and ease his transition from Farragut Academy to the NBA, and Garnett's mother moved to Minnesota for his first season. A *Star Tribune* reporter asked Blair how quickly Garnett would help the team: "That depends a lot on this," responded Blair as he pointed to his heart. "How quickly he will mature, nobody knows. A lot depends on how hard he wants to work."

New Jersey Nets assistant coach Jerry Eaves predicted that by Garnett's third year in the league, he "will be an absolute monster."

After the Wolves opened Garnett's rookie season with just six victories in their first twenty games, Saunders replaced Blair as coach. Saunders brought Garnett along slowly, easing him into a lineup that featured former number-one draft choices J. R. Rider and Christian Laettner. By midseason, Garnett had earned a spot in the starting lineup, making his first start on January 9 against the Los Angeles Lakers. Laettner was traded to the Atlanta Hawks a month later, and Rider was traded following the season, making Garnett the franchise's cornerstone.

As a rookie, Garnett averaged 10.4 points and 6.2 rebounds per game and was named to the NBA all-rookie second team. After this promising start, it was obvious that Garnett was the key to the team's future: with Garnett, the team that had won 15, 19, 20, and 21 games in the previous four seasons improved to 26 victories. And the next season, Garnett helped the Timberwolves reach the play-offs for the first time.

Eye Problems Force Puckett to Retire

*J*n 1996, Kirby Puckett started spring training with something to prove. A veteran of twelve major-league seasons, Puckett wanted to show that he was still the same player the team had known in previous years. On September 28, 1995, he had been hit on the left side of his face by a pitch from Cleveland's Dennis Martinez. Puckett suffered a fractured upper maxillary sinus, lacerations on the inside of his mouth, and two loose teeth, and these injuries forced him to miss the final three games of the season. In February, the thirty-five-year-old Puckett reported to the Twins' training camp in great shape and excited about returning to a potent Twins lineup, bolstered in the off-season by the signing of Paul Molitor. In his first nineteen spring training games, Puckett, who had a career .318 batting average, was 19-for-58 (.328).

On March 27, the Twins played host to the defending World Series champion Atlanta Braves in Fort Myers, Florida. A Hammond Stadium sellout crowd of 7,189 showed up to see Puckett and the Twins face Greg Maddux, winner of the National League Cy Young Award the previous four seasons. In four innings, Maddux allowed just two hits—one by Puckett—and one run. Puckett lined a single to right in the first inning but was robbed of a hit by Maddux in the third. After Maddux left the game, Puckett got another hit to improve his spring training average to .344 (21-for-61). Along with his improved batting average, at the end of spring training Puckett had two home runs and a team-high fourteen RBIs to prove he was completely recovered from his injuries.

On March 28, the Twins were scheduled to play their last exhibition game in Florida before flying to Denver for two exhibition games against the Colorado Rockies. Puckett, however, faced a drastic change of plans. That morning, he woke with blurred vision and a

Kirby Puckett's career with the Twins came to an abrupt end when he was diagnosed with glaucoma in 1996.

black dot in front of his right eye. After being examined by several Fort Myers eye doctors, who said the problem was unrelated to the injuries he had suffered six months earlier, Puckett flew to Baltimore to see a specialist at Johns Hopkins University. Puckett told the *Minneapolis Star Tribune,* "The doctor told me it could be a day, two days, a week, two weeks. But nothing can be done and I won't know anything more, until I see a specialist."

The initial diagnosis was that Puckett had a partially blocked blood vessel behind his right eye. On March 30, the Twins placed him on the fifteen-day disabled list for the first time in his career, but Puckett and the team were optimistic that he would miss just the first two weeks of the regular season. Their confidence dissolved on April 12, when tests at the Retina Institute of Maryland revealed that Puckett had an early form of glaucoma. Five days later he underwent laser surgery, and in early May doctors predicted that he had a fifty-fifty chance of regaining full vision in the eye. On May 11 Puckett took batting practice, and later that month doctors reported some improvement in his vision. But on May 28, he was transferred to the sixty-day disabled list.

In a span of ten days in mid-June, Puckett had two additional laser surgeries. Then, on July 12, Puckett again underwent surgery in Baltimore, where doctors reported that he had suffered irreversible damage to his retina. Puckett returned to the Twin Cities later that day and announced his retirement from baseball. Despite the misfortune, Puckett told the *Star Tribune,* "Baseball's been a great part of my life. But now it's time for me to close this chapter of this book in baseball and go on with Part II of my life. Kirby Puckett's going to be all right. Don't worry about me."

On September 8, as a crowd of fifty-one thousand filled the Hubert Humphrey Metrodome to honor Puckett, the Twins saluted him and retired his uniform number.

On the Road to the Final Four

Gophers Win 31 Games, Big Ten Title

After posting losing records in his first two seasons with the University of Minnesota basketball team, coach Clem Haskins saw the Gophers to the NCAA tournament in 1988–89. In his fourth season, the Gophers fell two points short of a trip to the NCAA Final Four, losing to Georgia Tech in the Southeast Regional championship game, 93–91. For the next six years, there was little postseason success, beyond a National Invitation Tournament championship in 1993. The Gophers went 1–1 in the NCAA tournament in 1994 and lost in the first round of the tournament in 1995. A year later, they went 1–1 in the NIT tournament.

The Gophers opened the 1996–97 season—Haskins's tenth as coach—with reason to be optimistic, returning all five starters—Eric Harris, Bobby Jackson, Sam Jacobson, Courtney James, and John Thomas—from the 1995–96 team, which had won twenty games and finished fifth in the Big Ten with a 10–8 record. Haskins told the *Minneapolis Star Tribune* that he thought the team had the talent to win the conference title. Setting out to prove themselves, the Gophers opened the season with victories over Stephen F. Austin and West Virginia before traveling to Puerto Rico for the San Juan Shootout. There the Gophers won three tournament games, including a championship victory over Clemson, to improve to 5–0.

Next, the Gophers suffered their first loss—at Alabama by three points. It was the only one for nearly six weeks as they won ten consecutive games—including a 114–34 victory over Alabama State for the largest margin of victory in school history—to improve their record to 15–1. The last four victories were over conference foes Wisconsin, Michigan State, Indiana (in overtime), and Michigan, but the winning streak ended on January 14 with a 96–90 loss at Illinois. Then the Gophers embarked on another successful run, emerging victorious

Guard Bobby Jackson led the Gophers in scoring for two seasons, averaging 15.3 points per game while helping the Gophers to a school-record 31 victories in 1996–97.

from their next twelve games to take a 27–2 overall record and 16–1 conference record into their regular-season finale at Wisconsin.

Despite a heartbreaking one-point loss to the Badgers, the Gophers claimed their first Big Ten title since 1982 and were rewarded with the number-one seed in the Midwest Regional. They opened the postseason on March 14 with a 78–46 victory over Southwest Texas State in Kansas City, and two days later the Gophers defeated Temple 76–57 to advance to the regional semifinals. On March 20, in San Antonio, they outlasted Clemson 90–84 in two overtimes. Then, in the Midwest Regional championship game, the Gophers rallied to defeat UCLA 80–72, earning the first trip to the NCAA Final Four in school history. The Gophers had trailed by ten points in the second half before taking the lead with an 11–0 run.

Arizona, North Carolina, and defending national champion Kentucky joined the Gophers in Indianapolis for the Final Four. After Arizona defeated North Carolina 66–58 in the first game on March 29, the Gophers and the Wildcats, coached by Rick Pitino, took the Hoosierdome floor for the second semifinal. Despite committing fifteen turnovers in the first twenty minutes, the Gophers trailed by just five points, 36–31, at halftime. In the second half, the Wildcats opened an eight-point lead, but the Gophers used a 9–0 run—with Jackson scoring the final

seven points—to go ahead 52–51 with 10:45 remaining. The Wildcats regrouped and eventually pulled away for a 78–69 victory. After being held to less than 40 percent shooting just three times during the season, the Wildcats shot 38 percent. Jackson outscored Kentucky All-American Ron Mercer, 23–19.

"A lot of things went wrong for us," Pitino explained to the *Star Tribune*. "They were very physical. They were dominating us in some ways." Jackson expressed his disappointment to the *Star Tribune,* "we wish we had the game back, but we can't."

Two days later, Arizona, coached by Minnesota native Lute Olson, defeated Kentucky 84–79 to win the national title.

The semifinal loss didn't diminish an extraordinary season for the Gophers, who earned a school-record 31 victories in 35 games and the sixth Big Ten title in school history. The day before the semifinal, Haskins was named the *Associated Press* Coach of the Year. His response: "I'm the same coach. I'm a good coach. I'm not any better or worse than I was 10 years ago. I just have better players now."

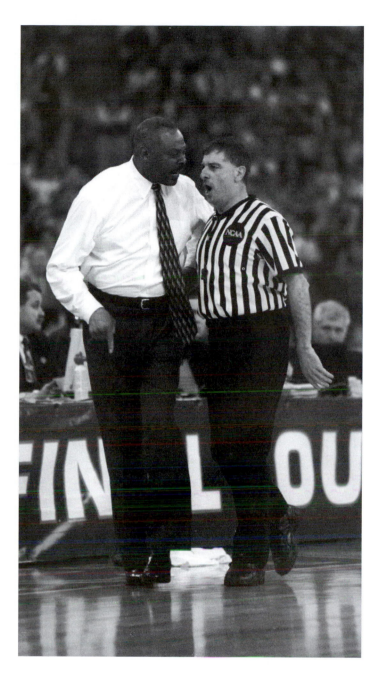

Clem Haskins coached the Gophers for thirteen seasons and in 1997 was named *Associated Press* Coach of the Year.

The Bubble Bursts

Vikings Season Ends Abruptly

A uthor Jules Renard once said, "There are moments when everything goes well; don't be frightened, it won't last." Unknowingly, with this statement the late-nineteenth-century writer foretold the Vikings' 1998 season.

After five play-off appearances in their first six years under Dennis Green, the Vikings were upbeat heading into the 1998 season. A 4–0 record in the preseason only fueled their optimism. The Vikings opened the regular season with seven consecutive victories, suffering their first loss on November 1, to the Tampa Bay Buccaneers, 27–24, in Tampa, Florida. The game's score was the lowest offensive output by the Vikings the entire season. Over the final eight regular-season weeks, they went 8–0 while scoring 291 points. In three of their final five games, they scored more than 45 points.

The 15–1 regular-season record earned the Vikings a first-round bye in the play-offs. They then blitzed Arizona 41–21 at the Metrodome to advance to their first National Football Conference championship game in eleven years. The extraordinary regular season had given Vikings fans high expectations for the play-offs, and many thought this was the team that would return to the Super Bowl for the first time in twenty years and avenge the franchise's four Super Bowl losses. One obstacle remained: the Atlanta Falcons. Like the Vikings, the Falcons had enjoyed a tremendous season: after going 3–13 the previous year, they had compiled a franchise-best 14–2 record.

With home-field advantage, the Vikings were installed as 11-point favorites over the Falcons. Odds-makers figured the Falcons would be unable to stop the Vikings' potent offense. Having scored an NFL-record 556 points, the Vikings were led offensively by quarterback

Randall Cunningham, who had joined the Vikings as a backup in 1997, passed for 3,937 yards and 35 touchdowns in 1998.

Randall Cunningham, who had passed for 3,704 yards and 34 touchdowns while throwing just 10 interceptions; running back Robert Smith, who had rushed for 1,187 yards and six touchdowns; rookie wide receiver Randy Moss, who had caught 69 passes for 1,313 yards and 17 touchdowns; and kicker Gary Anderson, who had been perfect the entire season, converting all 35 field-goal and 59 extra-point attempts.

"We understand that not many guys get this opportunity," Smith told the *Minneapolis Star Tribune*. "And to have this game at home, I mean this is it. We've said this from the beginning. There are no more excuses to be had. The organization has stepped up, re-signed all the players, brought in players. Everything's in place. It's just up to us now. This is our shot."

They missed their shot by one field goal.

The opening minutes were promising, as the Vikings created a 20–7 lead, but the Falcons took advantage of a turnover in the final moments of the first half to pull within 20–14 at intermission. The Vikings were able to push the lead back to ten points early in

Robert Smith, who rushed for 1,187 yards during the regular season, was one reason the Vikings reached the NFC championship game against Atlanta.

the fourth quarter, but the Falcons wouldn't relent. Leading 27–20 with just over two minutes remaining, the Vikings had a chance to open a ten-point lead, but Anderson missed a 38-yard field-goal attempt, his first failed kick of the season. The Falcons responded by going seventy-one yards in just eight plays—and seventy-eight seconds—to tie the game, capping the drive with Chris Chandler's 16-yard touchdown pass to Terance Mathis. The Vikings chose to run the clock out in the final minute of regulation, having Cunningham down the ball on a third-and-three situation from their own 27-yard line with thirty seconds remaining.

The Vikings won the coin toss going into the first conference and NFL championship game overtime since 1958. They had two possessions in the extra period, but the Vikings, who had amassed sixty-four touchdowns during the regular season, couldn't score. With three minutes and eight seconds remaining, Atlanta's Morten Andersen kicked a 38-yard field goal to complete the biggest upset in a conference championship game since the 1970 AFL-NFL merger.

The victory gave the Falcons their first Super Bowl berth in the franchise's thirty-three-year history. The loss left the high-scoring Vikings, who had managed just one touchdown after halftime, and their fans stunned. "We thought it was our year," Vikings cornerback Jimmy Hitchock told the *Star Tribune*. "It just didn't turn out that way. It was an unbelievable experience out there. I just never saw it coming like this. Never. I just feel empty."

The Vikings restocked and returned to the NFL play-offs the next two seasons, reaching the NFC championship game following the 2000 season.

March 10, 1999

ts: House Republicans rip Ventura's revised plan, depth of reductions   LOCAL, 1D

SAINT PAUL
MINNESOTA'S FIRST NEWSPAPER
CITY EDITION

PIONEER PRESS

150th ANNIVERSARY

© 1999 Saint Paul Pioneer Press (NorthWest Publication)

SDAY
30, NUMBER 318
erplanet.com

"I've been here 13 years. Don't you know me, what I stand for as a man, as a person? I haven't changed."
CLEM HASKINS, GOPHERS HEAD COACH

"I think it was more of a fact of laziness than it was of people really needing the help or really cheating to get by."
TREVOR WINTER, FORMER GOPHERS CENTER, ON WHY HE SAYS TEAMMATES HAD WORK DONE FOR THEM

hought I was going to actually
rn how to write a paper. I never
arned in high school. But then I sat
own and she just started typing."
RUSS ARCHAMBAULT,
FORMER GOPHERS GUARD

SPECIAL REPORT

U basketball program accused of academic fraud

Charge: At least 20 players had course work done by staff member

© 1999 St. Paul Pioneer Press

GEORGE DOHRMANN STAFF WRITER

A t least 20 men's basketball players at the University of Minnesota had research papers, take-home exams or other course work done for them during a five-year period, according to a former office manager in the academic counseling unit who said she did the work.

Four former players, Courtney James, Russ Archambault, Kevin Loge and Darrell Whaley, confirmed that work was prepared for them in possible violation of the student code of conduct and NCAA regulations. Another former player, Trevor Winter, said he was aware of the practice.

James, Archambault and the office manager, Jan Gangelhoff, said knowledge of the academic fraud was widespread.

"These are serious allegations," University of Minnesota President Mark Yudof said Tuesday. "We've called in legal counsel. I want to look into this promptly. But they are just allegations at this point." Gangelhoff, 50, said that from 1993 to 1998 she esti-

Editor's note

The Pioneer Press launched a three-month investigation into the academic counseling of the University of Minnesota's men's basketball players after learning the university had self-reported a violation to the NCAA.

CHARGE CONTINUED ON 6A

'Experiment': Haskins sought counselor's move to athletic staff

GEORGE DOHRMANN STAFF WRITER

H ow could an office manager in the University of Minnesota's academic counseling unit write papers and do take-home exams for basketball players for five years without being detected?

The answer, according to the university's retired academic counseling director, Elayne Donahue, stems from a pivotal decision made by top athletic department officials in October 1994 that took away any checks and balances for academic help for basketball players.

The decision was done at basketball coach Clem Haskins' request and approved by then-athletic director McKinley Boston. It moved Alonzo Newby, the academic counselor assigned to men's basketball, out of the university's academic counseling department and shifted him to the men's athletic department.

Of 22 sports at the university, the basketball team was the only one whose academic counselor did not report to Donahue.

The move — billed initially as an "experiment" to better help academically at-risk players, according to internal documents obtained by the Pioneer Press —

'EXPERIMENT' CONTINUED ON 7A ▶

INSIDE/ PAGE 9A
■ The NCAA does not take these kinds of allegations lightly. Tom Powers' column.
■ It's easy for students to get away with cheating in large classes, professors say.

A PLAYER

Former Gophers basketball player Courtney James confirmed that course work was prepared for him. One of the reports, on the Rev. Martin Luther King Jr. and Malcolm X, is shown at right.

MARTIN LUTHER KING, JR. AND MALCOLM X

The Same, or Different?

Submitted for

Afro 1011, Intro to Afro-American Studies

By

Courtney James

THE TUTOR

JEAN PIERI/PIONEER PRESS

"On the research papers, we would rarely meet. They would just give me the assignment and I would do it and then they would pick it up."
JAN GANGELHOFF
FORMER OFFICE MANAGER OF THE ACADEMIC COUNSELING UNIT

Former Gophers player Russ Archambault, shown here working with Jan Gangelhoff, said, "In the two years I was there, I never did a thing."

CORRESPONDENCE

Memo to McKinley Boston, vice president for athletics and student development: " ... It is becoming more apparent that I am just a front for whatever is going on in basketball's academic support program."
ELAYNE DONAHUE,
COUNSELING DIRECTOR
Memo dated Feb. 23, 1998

Letter to Jan Gangelhoff, former office manager: " ... Your involvement, unfortunately, has made it necessary for us to disassociate you from the men's basketball program."
MARK DIENHART,
DIRECTOR OF MEN'S ATHLETICS
Letter dated Oct. 26, 1998

Gopher Basketball Scandal Erupts

On "selection Sunday" 1999, some college basketball observers wondered if the University of Minnesota would be included in the 64-team NCAA tournament field. After finishing sixth in the Big Ten with an 8–8 regular-season record, the Gophers had suffered a three-point loss to last-place Illinois in the first round of the inaugural Big Ten postseason tournament. Surprisingly, the Gophers were named to the tournament field as the number seven seed in the West Regional. Traveling to Seattle, the Gophers braced themselves for questions about whether they belonged in the tournament.

But the questions they faced in Seattle were of an unexpected and more serious nature. Back home, the *St. Paul Pioneer Press* published a story that would render meaningless the Gophers' first-round game against Gonzaga. In its March 10 edition, the newspaper alleged that widespread academic fraud existed in the Gopher basketball program. The *Pioneer Press* report—covering five pages—asserted that a former office manager in the University's athletic academic counseling unit had completed—over a period of five years—more than four hundred assignments for at least twenty former and current Gopher men's basketball players. Four current team members were named in the report. If proven true, the allegations were quite serious, violating the University of Minnesota student conduct code and NCAA regulations.

Not unexpectedly, the story had an immediate impact. University president Mark Yudof cut short an out-of-state trip to return to Minneapolis. McKinley Boston, the University's vice president of student development and athletics, returned from Indianapolis where he

A three-month investigation into the University of Minnesota men's basketball program uncovered academic fraud and resulted in a Pulitzer Prize for the *St. Paul Pioneer Press.*

had been scheduled to serve as site manager for the NCAA tournament's South Regional. Yudof told the *Minneapolis Star Tribune,* "I was very disturbed by the allegations . . . there are lots of allegations and very serious ones. I guess my reaction was a great deal of sadness and worry, but I also have a lot of respect for Clem Haskins and for our program. I think I shouldn't jump to conclusions."

In Seattle, Haskins told the *Star Tribune,* "We are worried about one thing and that is our opponent."

The University's initial concern was the status of the four team members—including two starters—named in the report, as the administration had a little more than twenty-four hours to decide whether to revoke the four's eligibility for the game against Gonzaga. On the morning of March 11, the University declared Miles Tarver, Kevin Clark, Antoine Broxsie, and Jason Stanford ineligible. Hours later, the undermanned Gophers lost to the tenth-seeded Bulldogs, 75–63.

Three months later, on June 25, the University bought out Haskins's contract for $1.5 million. In July the Gophers hired a new coach—Dan Monson, who had coached Gonzaga to the victory over the Gophers. In November 1999, Yudof announced the findings of the school's internal investigation: the allegations were true. The school self-imposed penalties on the program, and eventually the NCAA placed the program on probation. The magnitude of the fraud stunned Minnesota and tarnished Haskins's previously stellar reputation.

June 12, 1999
Erasing a Memory

Women's Pro Basketball Returns as Lynx Debut

Unfortunately, the lingering memories of the Twin Cities' first women's professional basketball team had little to do with the game or the players. During three seasons in Minnesota, from 1978 to 1981, most of the news about the Fillies and the Women's Professional Basketball League centered on off-court issues—low attendance and unpaid bills [see pages 169–71].

When the newest women's basketball team tipped off in Minnesota in June 1999, it made a vastly different first impression. The franchise formed in April 1998 when the Women's National Basketball Association, which had debuted the previous summer and was owned collectively by the twenty-nine teams of the NBA, announced it would expand by two teams for the 1999 season. Franchises were awarded to Minnesota and Orlando with the condition that each team secure pledges for at least five thousand season tickets prior to September 1, 1998. The Minnesota team ably met its deadline, announcing it had surpassed six thousand season-ticket deposits.

Two weeks later, before it had hired a coach or chosen a nickname, the franchise was allocated its first player, Kristin Folkl of Stanford. Soon Brian Agler, who had coached Columbus to two titles in the winter-season rival American Basketball League, was named coach and general manager. The team selected four players in an expansion draft and five in the WNBA draft, but its most important player acquisition was Katie Smith, assigned to the

Katie Smith, who played at Ohio State and on the 1998 U.S. National team, was assigned to the Minnesota Lynx by the WNBA.

Women's professional basketball returned to Minnesota after an 18-year absence as the Lynx played host to the Detroit Shock at the Target Center on June 12, 1999.

franchise by the league. Smith had played at Ohio State and on the U.S. National team that won the 1998 World Championship gold medal and had also spent three seasons with Agler in Columbus. In fact, four other Lynx teammates had also played in Columbus.

"I think people around the league are saying two things," Agler told the *Minneapolis Star Tribune*. "They're saying, 'He just tried to transplant the team from Columbus to Minnesota,' and they're saying, 'They don't have enough height, quickness or scoring to have a lot of success in this league.'"

Indeed, one national publication didn't think much of the Lynx. *ESPN the Magazine* predicted the Lynx would finish last in their conference, noting: "Expansion Washington's 3–27 record from last year no longer looks so untouchable."

With something to prove, the Lynx opened training camp on May 14. In early June they traveled to Mankato to play their first exhibition game, an 80–76 loss to Orlando. Two days later, the same two teams met in Orlando, where the Miracle led by as many as 27 points during the game, winning 81–71. After these two tune-ups, the Lynx launched their inaugural regular season.

On June 12, the Lynx played host to the Detroit Shock at the Target Center. A crowd of 12,122 watched them defeat the Shock 68–51, becoming the first WNBA expansion team to win its debut. The previous season, the Shock went 17–13 and finished one victory shy of a play-off berth, but the Lynx limited them to 16 points in the first half. Lynx teammates Tonya Edwards (20), Brandy Reed (16), and Sonja Tate (12) combined for 48 points.

Edwards was moved by the experience, telling the *Minneapolis Star Tribune:* "I had tears in my eyes before the game started. It was great to see all those fans . . . We couldn't have written a better script for our first home game."

In their first season, the Lynx successfully transformed the legacy of the Twin Cities' first professional women's basketball team.

November 6, 1999
Gophers Get Their Kicks

Minnesota Upsets Number Two Penn State

The University of Minnesota football program had a brief and painful history with the Penn State Nittany Lions. For the teams' third meeting, in October 1997, the Gophers traveled to University Park, Pennsylvania, 34-point underdogs to number one–ranked Penn State. With ten minutes remaining in the game, the Gophers led 15–3. Five game minutes later the Gophers were ahead by five and had possession of the ball while Penn State had zero time-outs. But after recovering a Gopher fumble, the Nittany Lions rallied for a 16–15 victory. Following the game, Penn State coach Joe Paterno told the *Minneapolis Star Tribune* that the Gophers had deserved to win.

Two years later, the Gophers, now 0–4 against the Lions, again ventured to Penn State as underdogs. This time, the unbeaten and number two–ranked Nittany Lions were 14-point favorites. After opening the 1999 season with four consecutive victories, the Gophers took a 5–3 record into the contest at Penn State's Beaver Stadium. The numbers were stacked against them: in thirteen years, the Gophers had not defeated a top five–ranked team. Since 1991, the Gophers had won just four of thirty-three Big Ten Conference road games, two of those victories coming in 1991, against Northwestern and Illinois.

But these statistics were kicked aside by the Gophers and Dan Nystrom. All they needed were a few lucky bounces and six lead changes.

Penn State was ahead 7–3 after the first quarter before the Gophers took a 9–7 lead early in the second on a 25-yard touchdown pass from Billy Cockerham to Ron Johnson. But Nystrom missed the extra-point kick for the first time in thirty-four tries. Penn State scored late in the first half to regain the lead, the score 14–9 at halftime. Early in the third quarter, the Nittany Lions made it 17–9. But the Gophers pulled within two late in the quarter on a three-

Dan Nystrom's 32-yard field goal as time expired was the difference in the Gophers' one-point victory over the Nittany Lions in 1999.

yard touchdown run by Cockerham. The Gophers' try for a two-point conversion failed.

Penn State made it 20–15 on a 44-yard field goal by Travis Forney. Then the Gophers' Thomas Hamner, who had committed the crucial fumble in the loss to the Nittany Lions two years earlier, caught a 49-yard touchdown pass from Cockerham to give the Gophers a 21–20 lead with 11:25 remaining. The Gophers failed to convert another two-point attempt, and just two minutes later, Forney booted another 44-yard field goal to put the Nittany Lions ahead 23–21. Stopping the Gophers on their next possession, the Lions got the ball back, but after three consecutive scoring drives, on this one they were forced to punt. The kick, which sailed into the end zone, gave the Gophers the ball at their own 20-yard line with 1:50 remaining.

On the first play, Cockerham completed a 46-yard pass to Johnson, earning the Gophers a first down at the Nittany Lions' 34-yard line. Three plays later—after two incomplete passes and a six-

yard sack by All-American linebacker LaVar Arrington—the Gophers faced a fourth-and-sixteen situation at the Penn State 40. Cockerham heaved another desperation pass toward Johnson. As the ball bounced off Johnson's chest and appeared headed for the ground, Gopher receiver Arland Bruce made a heroic dive to catch the deflection, keeping the

Gophers' hopes alive with a first down at the 13. Three plays and one time-out later, Nystrom lined up for a 32-yard field goal. With most of the 96,753 spectators screaming for him to miss, the eighteen-year-old freshman booted the ball right down the middle as time expired, giving the Gophers a stunning 24–23 victory.

"I wanted a chance to make it up to my team by kicking the [winning] field goal," Nystrom told the *Minneapolis Star Tribune*. "I was nervous. You're always nervous in that situation, but I think I was prepared."

The Gopher football team celebrates a stunning come-from-behind 24–23 victory at Penn State in 1999.

The victory—their sixth of the season and their first over a top-five team since a 20–17 win against number two Michigan in November 1986—propelled the Gophers to their first winning season since 1990 and made them eligible for their first bowl game in thirteen years. For the Nittany Lions, it was just their third "homecoming" loss in thirty-four seasons under Paterno.

The Gophers closed out the regular season with a win at home over Indiana and a win at Iowa to finish with an 8–3 record, their first eight-victory season since 1961. Matching another mark from that year, the win over the Hawkeyes gave the Gophers a 4–0 record in conference road games for the first time since 1961. The 1999 season came to a disappointing end with a 24–20 loss to Oregon in the Sun Bowl in El Paso, Texas. Fittingly, the season's high point had been at Penn State, known to locals as "Happy Valley."

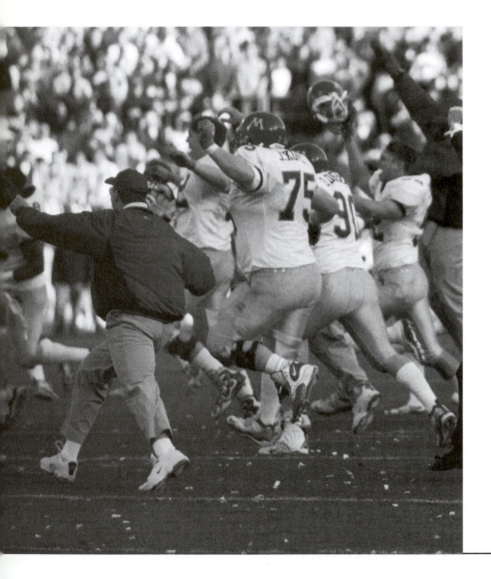

The Gopher football team celebrates at Penn State in 1999.

March 25, 2000
A National Title

Gopher Women's Hockey Team Wins Championship

After reaching the Final Four in the program's first two years, the University of Minnesota women's hockey team had to wait before finding out if there would be a third consecutive trip. On March 4, the Gophers lost to Minnesota-Duluth 2–0 in the championship game of the women's Western Collegiate Hockey Association tournament. The victory gave the Bulldogs, who had a 3–1–1 edge in the season series, the league's automatic bid to the American Women's College Hockey Alliance play-offs. The loss ended a 21-game winning streak for the Gophers and meant they would have to wait two weeks to see if their regular-season performance of 30–6–1 was enough to earn an at-large bid. In the end, the wait was well worth it.

Earning the at-large bid, the Gophers traveled to Boston for the tournament. Their uncertainty returned as on March 23, the day before their semifinal match against Minnesota-Duluth, their leading scorer, Nadine Muzerall, was injured in practice after a hard fall to the ice. Taken off the ice by stretcher, Muzerall was cleared to play just hours before the rematch with the Bulldogs. The Bulldogs opened a 2–0 lead, but Muzerall, who led the nation with 46 goals, scored twice to tie the game, and Tracy Engstrom made the tie-breaking goal with a little over six minutes remaining. The Gophers held on for a 3–2 victory, earning their first trip to the AWCHA championship game.

For the title, the Gophers faced Brown, the Eastern College Athletic Conference regular-season and tournament champion. Having won 18 of its previous 19 games, Brown was led by goalie Ali Brewer, who had recorded eleven shutouts during the season and was the recipient of the Patty Kazmaier award for the nation's top college player. In the championship game, Brown grabbed an early 1–0 lead, but the Gophers rallied for the second consecutive

day. Laura Slominski and Courtney Kennedy scored in the second period to put the Gophers ahead 2–1. A goal by Muzerall increased the Gophers' lead by one before Winny Brodt's goal—assisted by Muzerall—made it 4–1. Brown pulled within 4–2, but the Gophers and goalie Erica Killewald withstood the assault and held on for the national title. Killewald, who had made twenty-five saves in the semifinal victory, had thirty-four saves and was named the tournament's most valuable player.

"The last three weeks were the longest of the season," Killewald told the *Minneapolis Star Tribune*. "But we just stuck together. We practiced hard, we made it, played two great hockey games and won the national championship. It doesn't get any better than that."

Coach Laura Halldorson, who had directed the Gophers to records of 21–7–3 and 29–4–3 in their first two varsity seasons, agreed: "Our team showed a lot of character this weekend. We stuck together as a team."

That teamwork helped the Gophers quickly ascend to the forefront of college women's hockey and gave the University of Minnesota two championship-caliber ice hockey teams.

In just their third season as a varsity sport, the Gopher women's hockey team claimed the 2000 national championship.

October 11, 2000
Hockey Comes Home

Minnesota Wild Battle Flyers in Their First Game

Almost immediately after the North Stars relocated to Dallas in spring 1993 [see pages 209–11], people in the Twin Cities started exploring ways to lure the National Hockey League back to Minnesota. Initially, their efforts centered on acquiring an existing franchise. Just six months after the North Stars played their final game at the Met Center, NHL commissioner Gary Bettman announced that the Edmonton Oilers were considering relocating to Minneapolis and playing in the Target Center. Then, in April 1995, the Winnipeg Jets said they were contemplating a new home in Minnesota. Two months later, the Jets decided to remain in Winnipeg for the 1995–96 season, and in December 1995 the Jets announced their move—to Phoenix.

In November 1996, after the Oilers and Jets had spurned the state, a Minnesota group formally applied for an NHL expansion team, joining eight other interested cities—Atlanta, Columbus, Houston, Nashville, Norfolk, Oklahoma City, Raleigh-Durham, and Hamilton (Ontario). In April 1997, Bettman and other NHL officials toured the St. Paul Civic Center to assess its suitability for a future team. Finding the facility inadequate, Bettman told St. Paul mayor Norm Coleman that the city would need a new arena if it hoped to land a franchise. St. Paul, which had been considering a $51 million renovation of the Civic Center—home to the Fighting Saints of the 1970s World Hockey Association—quickly developed a financing package for a $130 million arena on the Civic Center site.

Two months after Bettman's visit, another existing NHL franchise, the Hartford Whalers, flirted with the Twin Cities before announcing it would relocate to North Carolina instead of Minnesota. A month later, the NHL expansion committee recommended that St. Paul be awarded an expansion team, and on June 25 the league's board of governors

After a seven-year absence, the NHL returned to Minnesota when the Wild played host to the Philadelphia Flyers at St. Paul's Xcel Energy Center on October 11, 2000.

approved Robert Naegele Jr.'s investment group for the franchise. The team would begin play in the 2000–2001 season.

"When we came on our site visit and we looked at the Civic Center," Bettman told the *Star Tribune*. "We thought they were dead in the water. We had some candid conversations, and Mayor Coleman said: 'We're going to get this done,' and he did."

Before the NHL formally returned to Minnesota, the transplanted Dallas Stars played an exhibition at the Target Center. On September 30, 1998, a crowd of 18,294—the largest to attend an NHL game in Minnesota—watched Phoenix defeat the Stars 2–1.

The expansion Minnesota Wild—their name chosen from six finalists that included

Blue Ox, Northern Lights, Freeze, Voyageurs, and White Bears—played their first preseason game on September 19, 2000, skating to a 3–3 tie with San Jose in Portland, Oregon. Ten days later, the Wild christened their new arena—the Xcel Energy Center—with a 3–1 victory over Anaheim. Those two teams opened the regular season in Anaheim on October 6, with the Mighty Ducks winning 3–1.

On October 11, 2000—after a seven-and-one-half-year absence—the NHL officially returned to Minnesota as the Wild played their first regular-season home game, against the Philadelphia Flyers. Before a crowd of 18,827, the Wild led 2–1 and 3–2 before settling for a tie after Eric Desjardins scored for the Flyers midway through the third period. "The thing I like the best was we kept coming back," Wild coach Jacques Lemaire told the

From the beginning, fans have embraced the return of the NHL to the state. The Wild sold out each home game in its first three seasons.

Star Tribune. "We never gave up, and we battled the whole way. I could tell the guys were nervous at the start of the game. That was expected because it was the first game and all. But then they settled down."

Even more memorable for Wild fans was the first Minnesota goal—scored by Richfield's Darby Hendrickson. "Who knows, maybe a hundred years from now, people will talk about Darby scoring that first goal—you know, a local guy," Wild forward and former Gopher Jeff

Nielsen told the *Star Tribune*. "And I got a point. To have that happen in the first game was almost perfect. It would've been perfect if we could've won, but tying a pretty good team like Philadelphia makes it pretty special."

A mere two and one-half years later, the Wild would qualify for the play-offs, becoming just the third NHL team since 1970 to do so in its third year of existence.

January 16, 2001
Favorite Sons Enshrined

Winfield, Puckett
Enter Baseball Hall of Fame

One is arguably the most gifted all-around athlete to come out of Minnesota. The other was told that he was too small to play in the major leagues. But what St. Paul native Dave Winfield and Chicago-born Kirby Puckett have in common is a love of baseball. In January 2001 they shared something else: selection to the Baseball Hall of Fame.

The only athlete to be drafted by teams in three professional sports, the six-foot-six Winfield played basketball and baseball at the University of Minnesota. After helping the Gophers earn a third-place finish in the 1973 College World Series, Winfield, who had been drafted by professional basketball, football, and baseball teams, went directly to the major leagues. He was the fourth player selected in baseball's annual amateur draft and made his major-league debut with the San Diego Padres two weeks later. Winfield went on to compile 3,110 hits, 465 home runs, and 1,833 RBIs for six teams in a 22-year major-league career. He is one of only seven players in major-league history with at least 3,000 hits and 400 home runs.

The five-foot-eight Puckett spent a little over two seasons in the minor leagues before his 1984 major-league debut with the Minnesota Twins. He tied a record by getting four hits in his first game. After this auspicious start, Puckett pounded out 2,040 hits in his first ten full major-league seasons—the second-most in baseball history, trailing only Willie Keeler's

Dave Winfield, left, and Kirby Puckett share a laugh following their induction into the National Baseball Hall of Fame. Winfield and Puckett won election in their first year of eligibility.

2,065 hits. He contributed to the Twins' World Series victories in 1987 and 1991. Before being forced into premature retirement because of eye problems, he compiled 2,304 hits and a .318 career batting average and was a ten-time all-star during twelve major-league seasons.

Winfield and Puckett's paths converged in 1993 when they were teammates for the Twins. On September 16, Puckett was on third base when Winfield singled to left off Oakland's Dennis Eckersley for his 3,000th career hit.

They both concluded their careers following the 1995 season. To be considered for the Hall of Fame, a player has to be retired at least five years, and for election the player must be named on 75 percent of the ballots submitted by members of the Baseball Writers Association of America. Winfield and Puckett became eligible following the 2000 season, and when the poll results were announced on January 16, 2001, Winfield was named on 435 of 515 ballots while Puckett was named on 423—both easily exceeding the 387 required.

They became the thirty-fifth and thirty-sixth players (out of 254) to be elected in their first year of eligibility. Winfield was just the second Minnesota-born major-leaguer—after Chief Bender—and Puckett was the third youngest—behind Lou Gehrig and Sandy Koufax—to be voted into the Hall of Fame. They joined former Twins Harmon Killebrew, Rod Carew, and Steve Carlton. Puckett is the only one of the group who spent his entire career with the Twins.

Asked by the *Minneapolis Star Tribune* why he thought he qualified for the Hall on the first ballot, Winfield said, "I would assume that a constant high level of play over a couple of decades is one reason."

In addition to physical ability, Puckett stood out for another reason. Former Twins general manager Andy MacPhail told the *Star Tribune*'s Dan Barreiro, "no matter what the profession, people like the idea of someone who enjoys what they are doing, that it's not a labor. In so many ways, professional athletes are living the dream of the average guy. Yet so many athletes today seem to approach everything they do as if it is a terrible imposition, as if every day is a battle. Kirby conveyed just the opposite. He let everybody know that he was having fun playing the game. He was a beacon for baseball at a time when the game needed it."

Winfield, a native Minnesotan, and Puckett, the adopted son who was named number one in the *Star Tribune*'s Top 100 Minnesota Sports Figures for the twentieth century, shared the spotlight at the induction ceremonies at the Baseball Hall of Fame in Cooperstown, New York.

Gopher Men's Hockey Team Claims Title

Too much success in college athletics can breed unreasonable expectations. Any season that doesn't end in a national championship is a letdown for fans of legendary programs like University of Kentucky men's basketball, University of Nebraska football, University of Iowa wrestling, and University of Tennessee women's basketball. When one considers past performance to be a predictor of future success, the University of Minnesota men's hockey program is an example of the adage "it is sometimes easier to reach the pinnacle of a sport than it is to stay there."

One of the nation's most successful and visible college hockey programs, the Gophers won three national titles in a six-year span in the 1970s under coach Herb Brooks. The third title in that brief dynasty came in 1979, but beginning the next year the Gophers embarked on a lengthy national-title drought. Between 1980 and 2001, the Gophers played in the NCAA tournament fifteen times, reaching the tournament semifinals eight times but the championship game only once, finishing second in 1989.

Doug Woog, the winningest coach in school history, guided the Gophers to the Final Four six times during a 14-season span beginning in 1985. Failing to win a national championship, he was asked to step aside following the 1999 season. The task of winning a national title was handed to Minnesota native Don Lucia, who had coached Colorado College to three Western Collegiate Hockey Association championships and four appearances in the NCAA tournament in the previous six seasons. In Lucia's second season with the program, 2000–2001, the Gophers finished third in the WCHA—their best league finish in four years—and reached the NCAA play-offs. Their first NCAA appearance in four years ended abruptly with a 5–4 overtime loss to Maine, but it was the light at the end of the tunnel for Gopher hockey fans.

The Gophers opened the 2001–02 season with a mix of talented upperclassmen—forward John Pohl, forward Jeff Taffe, defenseman Jordan Leopold, and goalie Adam Hauser—and a highly regarded freshman class, all of whom quickly displayed their potential. Following a 7–5 exhibition victory over North Dakota—the first game in Grand Forks' Ralph Engelstad Arena—the Gophers opened the regular season with an 11-game unbeaten streak: ten victories and a tie. Their momentum slowed over the middle one-third of the schedule, as they won just seven of sixteen games (7–7–2), but following a 5–2 loss to Minnesota-Duluth on February 1, the Gophers were nearly perfect over the final two months of the season, winning eight of their final nine regular-season games and wrapping up the regular season with two victories over St. Cloud State. Their only loss in that span was to Colorado College.

The Gophers won two games over North Dakota to advance to the WCHA Final Five at the Xcel Energy Center in St. Paul. There they defeated St. Cloud State 4–1 in the semifinals, but regular-season champion Denver temporarily slowed the Gophers with a 5–2 victory in the championship game. After a first-round bye in the NCAA West Regional at Ann Arbor, Michigan, the Gophers defeated Colorado College 4–2 to earn a spot in the Frozen Four, scheduled to be played in their backyard—at St. Paul's Xcel Energy Center.

On April 4, the Gophers defeated Michigan 3–2, advancing to the NCAA title game for the first time since 1988. Two nights later, before 19,324 spectators—the largest crowd to see a hockey game in Minnesota—the Gophers and Maine squared off for the national title. Keith Ballard staked the Gophers to a 1–0 lead, but Maine tied the score in the second period. Just fifty-one seconds after the Black Bears had evened the score, Pohl put the Gophers ahead 2–1. Maine again tied the score and then took the lead with less than five minutes remaining. As time ran out on their title hopes, the Gophers pulled Hauser for an extra skater, and then, with just fifty-three seconds remaining, Matt Koalska scored the tying goal. The rejuvenated Gophers needed only three overtime minutes before Grant Potulny scored the game winner.

"At the start of the year, this was all we talked about," Lucia told the *Minneapolis Star Tribune*. "It was our time. I'm so proud of my players. We are all going to remember this day the rest of our lives. It's the most incredible feeling I've ever had."

Potulny, the only non-Minnesotan on the Gophers' roster—hailing from Grand Forks, North Dakota—agreed: "This was such a long time coming. I can't tell you how great this feels for everyone."

A review of the Gophers' first championship in twenty-three years reveals many highlights. As a team they had shown their resilience, going the entire season without losing two consecutive games. Individually, Leopold, who broke the school's single-season record for goals by a defenseman with 20, and Pohl, who finished as the nation's leading scorer with 27 goals and 52 assists, were named first-team All-American. Leopold also became the fourth player in school history to win the Hobey Baker Award, college hockey's top individual prize.

The national title was the second in a month for the University of Minnesota: in March, the Gopher wrestling team had won its second consecutive title. And the athletic department wasn't finished: two months later, the Gopher men's golf team—targeted for elimination early in the season to cut costs—won a national title. University of Minnesota sports fans, accustomed to quality athletic teams, had probably just witnessed the most memorable year in school history.

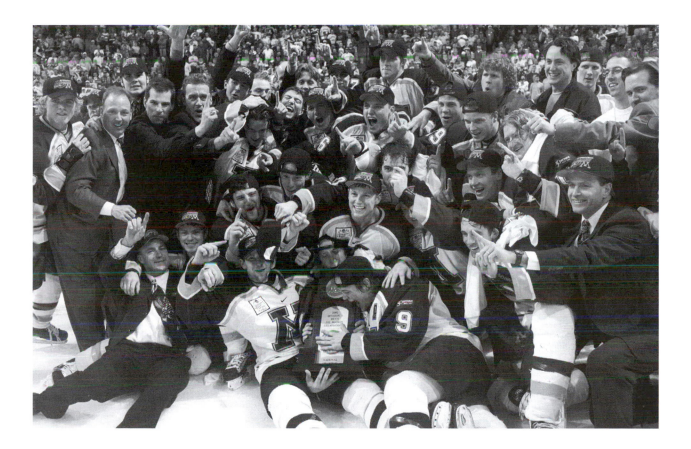

The Gopher hockey team celebrates the 2002 NCAA championship, the program's first in twenty-three years.

Ron Gardenhire, a Twins coach for eleven
seasons, directed the team to its first division title
in twelve years during his first season as manager.

A Second Chance

Twins, Threatened with Contraction, Win Division

The Minnesota Twins appeared to hit rock bottom in 1999. Just eight years removed from a World Series championship, but following six consecutive losing seasons—including back-to-back 90-loss seasons in 1997 and 1998—the Twins started the rebuilding process all over again. Their 1999 team—seventeen rookies on a twenty-five-man roster—had the lowest payroll in major league baseball at $16.4 million. Perhaps not unexpectedly, the result was another 90-loss season.

But even those ninety-seven losses were not the organization's lowest point, which came two years later. The nadir of the Twins' existence in Minnesota occurred in November 2001, just two days after the World Series, when commissioner Bud Selig announced that major league baseball intended to "contract" two teams, targeting the Minnesota Twins and the Montreal Expos. Twins owner Carl Pohlad, praised for keeping the team in Minnesota after he purchased the franchise from Calvin Griffith in 1984, apparently agreed that receiving a check for folding the franchise was better than the annual budget losses and the ongoing fight for a new stadium.

But before Major League Baseball could put its plan in motion, a legal obstacle emerged. On November 16, just ten days after the contraction issue had been broached, Hennepin County district court judge Harry Crump issued an injunction that forced the team to honor its 2002 lease in the Metrodome. Major League Baseball challenged Crump's decision, but the Minnesota Court of Appeals upheld it on January 22, 2002. The contraction plans were dropped, at least temporarily, on February 5, after the state's supreme court refused to hear the case.

Given a reprieve, the Twins flourished in 2002. Coming off a respectable 2001 season—eighty-five victories, their first winning season since 1992—they had reason to be optimistic. And with an 18–14 spring-training record, the Twins showed they would be competi-

Eddie Guardado saved 45 games during the regular season and two in the play-offs in his first season as the Twins closer.

tive in the American League Central. In fact, after holding first or second place for the first fifty games, the Twins moved into the top spot permanently on May 27. At the season's midpoint, they were 45–36, and they went 19–7 in July to open a 14-game lead in the standings.

But the Twins' drive to a division championship wasn't without drama. In mid-August, the Major League Baseball Players Association set a strike date of August 30 if a new collective bargaining agreement wasn't reached with the owners. A work stoppage would not only put the Twins' season in jeopardy; it would also threaten the franchise's existence. The strike was averted when players and owners reached an agreement on a new four-year contract just hours before the union's deadline. The new deal put off contraction until at least 2007, giving the Twins time to finalize plans for a new stadium.

Back on the field, the Twins defeated the Cleveland Indians 5–0 on September 15 to clinch their first division title in ten years—the earliest clinching date of the Twins' six league or division championship teams. They closed the regular season with five victories in their final six games, finishing with ninety-four wins and earning the right to play the A.L. West champion Oakland Athletics in the A.L. division series. The Athletics, who won 103 regular-season games, were favorites against the Twins, who had spent 157 days in first place during the 2002 season.

On October 1, the Twins opened the series with a 7–5 win over the Athletics in Oakland. The Athletics evened the best-of-seven series with a 9–1 victory the next day, but the Twins won the next three games, closing out the series with a breathtaking 5–4 victory in Oakland on October 6. Leading 2–1 going into the ninth, the Twins scored three insurance runs, but they had to hang on as the Athletics scored three in the bottom of the inning before pitcher Eddie Guardado was able to save the victory.

The Twins advanced to the American League Championship Series against the A.L. West runner-up Anaheim Angels, who had surprised the favored New York Yankees in the other division series. On October 8, the Twins continued their streak with a 2–1 victory over the Angels in game one at the Metrodome, behind the pitching of Joe Mays and Guardado, who combined on a four-hitter before 55,562 spectators. But the Angels evened the series the next night with a 6–3 victory at the Metrodome and went on to win three straight in Anaheim, earning their first trip to the World Series. The Angels punctuated the series with a 13–5 victory in game five on October 13.

The loss didn't tarnish the Twins' outstanding season, during which outfielder Torii

All-Star Torii Hunter led the Twins in home runs, RBIs, and stolen bases during the 2002 regular season.

Hunter emerged as one of the top players in the American League. Hunter, who dazzled a national audience with a remarkable catch in the All-Star Game, led the Twins with 29 home runs, 94 RBIs, and 23 stolen bases and earned his second Gold Glove award. With their 94–67 record, the Twins' season was remarkable—especially considering the drama that had swirled around Major League Baseball during the previous twelve months.

Afterword

Whenever I mention this book, people ask which of the 75 events I consider to be the most important. My answer, which isn't meant to be trite or evasive, is all of them. Being a sports fan is a subjective experience; my challenge was to be objective, to select events based on their significance in their own eras and their lasting impact. It didn't surprise me to learn that Minnesotans were just as passionate about sports one hundred years ago as they are today (see, for example, the chapters on Dan Patch and Pudge Heffelfinger). I quickly realized that trying to rank all these events, with their different eras, various sports, and distinctive heroes, would be an exercise in futility.

It's also difficult to put an end date on a project like this. After I completed the first draft in summer 2002, Minnesota sports fans continued to be entertained by remarkable events. Of course, we'll need the distance of history in order to judge whether these moments are truly memorable in the scheme of things. But here's a sample:

In August 2002, unheralded Rich Beem and Tiger Woods dazzled a crowd of forty thousand during the final round of the PGA Championship at Hazeltine National Golf Club in Chaska. Beem held off Woods, who birdied the last four holes and shot a final-round 67, for a one-stroke victory and his first major tournament championship.

In March 2003, the University of Minnesota women's basketball team, led by the All-American guard Lindsay Whalen, participated in the NCAA postseason for the second consecutive year. The Gophers and Whalen surprised Stanford to reach the tournament's round of sixteen before losing to highly ranked Texas.

The following month, the University of Minnesota men's hockey team won its second consecutive national title. The Gophers were led by freshman Thomas Vanek, who scored thirty-one goals during the season and was named the most outstanding player of the Final Four.

The Timberwolves 2002–03 season included Kevin Garnett's inspirational, MVP-caliber play and was capped by a play-off series against the Los Angeles Lakers. Garnett averaged a career-high 23 points, 13.4 rebounds, and 6 assists per game and had at least 10 points and 10 rebounds in 68 of the team's 82 regular-season games. The Timberwolves took a 2–1 lead in the play-off series before falling 4–2 to the defending NBA champion Lakers.

Finally, I would be remiss if I didn't mention the extraordinary 2003 play-off run by the Minnesota Wild. In just their third season and with the lowest payroll in the NHL, the Wild reached the Western Conference finals by rallying from a 3–1 deficit in each of their first two play-off series. The upstart Wild upset the Colorado Avalanche and goalie Patrick Roy in the first round and the physical Vancouver Canucks in the second, but their dreams of playing in the Stanley Cup finals were dashed by the Anaheim Mighty Ducks.

Sports fans in Minnesota are fortunate, for the four "major" professional sports franchises and a noteworthy college athletic program, all located in the Twin Cities, together offer a constant source for memorable events. The stories related in this book were gathered from nearly 150 years of Minnesota history. Just imagine what memorable moments lie ahead in the next ten, fifty, or 150 years.

Bibliography

BOOKS AND ARTICLES

Barton, George. *My Lifetime in Sports*. Minneapolis: Olympic Press, 1957.

The Baseball Encyclopedia, 10th Edition. New York: Macmillan Publishing, 1996.

Bernstein, Ross. *Frozen Memories: Celebrating a Century of Minnesota Hockey*. Minneapolis: Nodin Press, 1999.

———. *Hardwood Heroes: Celebrating a Century of Minnesota Basketball*. Minneapolis: Nodin Press, 2001.

———. *Pigskin Pride: Celebrating a Century of Minnesota Football*. Minneapolis: Nodin Press, 2000.

Brown, George E. III. *100 Years of Minnesota Golf: Our Great Tradition*. Edina, Minn.: Minnesota Golf Association, Inc., 2001.

Diamond, Dan, James Duplacey, Igor Kuperman, and Eric Zweig, eds. *Total Hockey: The Official Encyclopedia of the National Hockey League*. Kingston, N.Y.: Total Sports Publishing, 1998.

Greiner, Tony, comp. *The Minnesota Book of Days: An Almanac of State History*. St. Paul: Minnesota Historical Society Press, 2001.

Johnson, Lloyd, ed. *The Minor League Register*. Durham, N.C.: Baseball America, Inc., 1994.

Kelley, James. *Minnesota Golf: 90 Years of Tournament History*. Edina, Minn.: Minnesota Golf Association, Inc., 1991.

Kirchoff, Maggie, ed. *Let's Play Hockey Presents a Complete History of the Minnesota Boys & Girls High School Hockey Tournament, 1945–2000*. Minneapolis: D&M Publishing, Inc., 2000.

Lannin, Joanne. *A History of Basketball for Girls and Women: From Bloomers to the Big Leagues*. Minneapolis: Lerner Publishing Group, 2000.

Lazenby, Roland. *The Lakers: A Basketball Journey*. Indianapolis, Ind.: The Master's Press, 1995.

McClellan, Keith. *The Sunday Game: At the Dawn of Professional Football*. Akron, Ohio: The University of Akron Press, 1998.

Monroe, Cecil O. "The Rise of Baseball in Minnesota." *Minnesota History* 19 (1938): 162–81.

Neft, David S., Richard M. Cohen, and Rick Korch. *The Football Encyclopedia: The Complete History of Professional Football from 1892 to the Present*. New York: St. Martin's Press, 1991.

O'Neal, Bill. *The American Association: A Baseball History, 1902–1991*. Austin, Tex.: Eakin Publications, 1992.

Perlstein, Steve, ed. *Gopher Glory: 100 Years of University of Minnesota Basketball*. Minneapolis: Layers Publishing, 1995.

Pfaender, John A. *The First Hundred Years at the Town and Country Club*. St. Paul: Town & Country, 1988.

Salin, Tony. *Baseball's Forgotten Heroes: One Fan's Search for the Game's Most Interesting Overlooked Players*. Chicago: Masters Press, 1999.

Schofield, Mary Halverson. *Henry Boucha: Star of the North*. Edina, Minn.: Snowshoe Press, 1999.

Thornley, Stew. *On to Nicollet: The Glory and Fame of the Minneapolis Millers*. Minneapolis: Nodin Press, 1988.

THIS BOOK INCLUDES INFORMATION FROM ARTICLES
PUBLISHED IN THE FOLLOWING NEWSPAPERS:

The Duluth News-Tribune

The Emigrant Aid Journal

The Fairmont Sentinel

The Minneapolis Journal

The Minneapolis Star

The Minneapolis Star Journal

The Minneapolis Star Tribune

The Minneapolis Tribune

The Minnesota Daily

The St. Paul Daily News

The St. Paul Dispatch

The St. Paul Pioneer Press

THIS BOOK RELIED ON THE MEDIA GUIDES
FOR THE FOLLOWING TEAMS AND ORGANIZATIONS:

The Dallas Stars

The Ladies Professional Golf Association

The Los Angeles Lakers

The Minnesota Timberwolves

The Minnesota Twins

The Minnesota Vikings

The Minnesota Wild

The University of Minnesota baseball, football, men's basketball, men's hockey, and women's hockey

Photo Credits

Page 5	Image courtesy Transcendental Graphics, Boulder, Colorado
Pages 14, 17, 18	Courtesy University of Minnesota Archives
Pages 20, 21, 43, 56, 60, 64, 86, 106, 107, 150, 151, 152, 154, 182, 183, 226, 227, 238, 239, 240, 242, 251	
	Courtesy University of Minnesota Athletics
Pages 38, 68, 94, 96, 98, 104, 120, 164, 214	
	Courtesy Star Tribune
Page 39	Reprinted by permission of the *Duluth News Tribune*
Pages 40, 62, 65, 232	Photos courtesy Pioneer Press
Pages 53, 84	Photos courtesy *The Minnesota Daily*
Pages 80, 82	Private collection
Pages 92, 132, 156	Minnesota Vikings
Pages 95, 172, 174, 211	AP/Wide World Photos
Pages 108, 110	Photos by Buzz Magnuson/MHS Collections
Pages 111, 112, 114, 138, 140, 166, 168, 178, 191, 194, 195 (top and bottom), 204, 205, 206, 224, 252, 254, 255	Courtesy Minnesota Twins
Page 124	Photo by Flynn Eli/MHS Collections
Pages 125, 126, 129, 134, 136	Photos by Spence Hollstadt/MHS Collections
Pages 128, 158	Photos by John Croft/MHS Collections
Pages 137, 143, 144, 146, 148 (top and bottom)	
	Photos by Neale Van Ness/MHS Collections
Page 159	Photo by Bruce Bisping/MHS Collections
Page 160	Photo by Steve Schluter/MHS Collections
Page 171	Photo by Pete Hohn, courtesy Star Tribune
Pages 176, 184, 186, 187, 246	Photos by John Doman, Pioneer Press
Page 177	Photo by Spence Hollstadt, Pioneer Press
Pages 196, 198, 208, 228, 230	Courtesy Minnesota Vikings and Rick Kolodziej
Pages 200, 202, 222	Photos courtesy Minnesota Timberwolves
Page 210	Photo by Bill Alkofer, Pioneer Press
Page 212	Copyright © USGA/by Robert Walker
Pages 216, 218, 219	Photos by Jean Pieri, Pioneer Press
Pages 220, 234, 236	Photos courtesy David Sherman/Minnesota Timberwolves
Pages 244, 245	Courtesy Bruce Kluckhohn/Minnesota Wild

All other images are from the Minnesota Historical Society's collections.

Index